779
LIF/One
219

6176

entered

# LIFE THE '60S

# LIFE THE '60S

Edited by DORIS C. O'NEIL

Introduction by TOM BROKAW
Commentary by JOHN NEARY

A BULFINCH PRESS BOOK · LITTLE, BROWN AND COMPANY

Boston Toronto London

First Edition

Library of Congress Cataloging-in-Publication Data

Life — the '60s/edited by Doris C. O'Neil; introduction by Tom
    Brokaw; commentary by John Neary.
        p.   cm.
        "A Bulfinch Press book."
        ISBN 0-8212-1752-6
        1. United States — History — 1961–1969 — Pictorial works. 2. United
States — Civilization — 1945 – — Pictorial works. 3. History,
Modern — 1945 – — Pictorial works. I. O'Neil, Doris C. II. Neary,
John, 1937 – . III. Life (Chicago, Ill.) IV. Title: Life — the
Sixties.
E841.L54 1989
973.92 — dc20                                                89-7964
                                                                CIP

Bulfinch Press is an imprint and trademark of
Little, Brown and Company (Inc.).
Published simultaneously in Canada by
Little, Brown & Company (Canada) Limited.

Designed by Carl Zahn
Edited by Janet Swan Bush
Copyedited by Fredrica A. Harvey

PRINTED IN THE UNITED STATES OF AMERICA

# CONTENTS

CONTENTS

# PREFACE

The sixties had enough important stories to fill a half century: civil rights, women's lib, hippies, rock music, drugs, the sexual revolution, and the Vietnam War. These years produced some of the most unforgettable photographs the world has ever seen. In addition, the stories behind most of these photographs are equally important and unforgettable. The book begins with the civil rights movement and its horrors and struggles, which ultimately worked to bring us together. It ends with the Vietnam War and the agonies that tore us apart.

This book grew out of the exhibition and catalog "LIFE: Through the Sixties," sponsored by United Technologies Corporation and LIFE magazine. The exhibition was the third in a series that reviewed, usually in ten-year segments, the photographs assigned or gathered by LIFE in the course of its thirty-six-year career as a weekly magazine. The years covered by this exhibition were from 1956 through 1972. In editing the exhibition for this book, most of the photographs from the fifties and seventies were eliminated, and nearly one hundred additional photographs from the sixties were added.

There are over 250,000 images in LIFE's Picture Collection for the period covered by this book. It is a file of such richness that it required more than three years for me to look at each of those images and to make the difficult choices shown here. In some instances, the choice was an obvious one; but in most cases, the outstanding quality of the thousands of photographs available made the final choice a very difficult one.

Many of the photographs here could have been taken only in the sixties. They are illustrations of the agitation, unrest, and protest that was building at many levels of life and in many parts of the world. Some, however, illustrate emotions that are always part of life in any period—joy, grief, fear, love, compassion.

Despite the horrors of these times—or maybe because of them—one emotion dominated all others in the words spoken or written during this period. The emotion that most people who lived through the sixties would unhesitatingly associate with those years was love. A love for all mankind; a love to be sung about, usually to the accompaniment of a guitar; and a love to be lived out, sometimes in a commune. Much of the spirit of the decade has vanished, but thanks to the fact that those times did happen, one can talk about love, even today, without being thought of as odd.

May these photographs help to keep that extraordinary time always alive.

DORIS C. O'NEIL
*Director of Vintage Prints*, LIFE

# INTRODUCTION

Here it is almost the nineties and I'm *still* trying to figure out the sixties. There are so many vivid memories of that bizarre, whacked-out, depressing, exhilarating, moving, confusing time, I wonder, Was this a dream, an extended psychotic episode, some kind of cosmic journey? What were we doing and what did it all mean?

The answer to the first question is no and yes. No, it was not a dream. Yes, we did somehow muddle through, most of us anyway. The answer to the second question is more complex. The sixties had so many parts, so many beginnings without endings, so many convulsions it is impossible to get a uniform judgment of exactly what it was we went through. There is no consensus, not even within tribal subsets forged by what they believed at the time were common interests.

It was an era of dizzying contradictions. These were just some of the people, events, and passing fancies competing for our attention: John and Robert Kennedy; Richard Nixon; Martin Luther King, Jr.; George Wallace; H. Rap Brown; General William Westmoreland; Tom Hayden; William F. Buckley; Betty Friedan; Phyllis Schlafly; César Chavez; Ronald Reagan; the Beatles, the Supremes, Janis Joplin, Bob Dylan, and Julie Andrews; long hair, short shorts, tie-dyed shirts, and hard hats; tune in, turn on, drop out, and Jesus Loves You; Woodstock and Kent State; Americans on the moon and Americans in Vietnam.

If you mark the beginning of the decade, as I do, with the assassination of John F. Kennedy and the end of it with the resignation of Richard Nixon in 1974, you're out of sync with the calendar but in sync with the flow of events that so set the decade apart, the mention of any one of them prompting people to pause now, shake their head, and say softly, "Yeah, the sixties." Kennedy's election, which coincided with the chronological start of the decade, promised a new era of youthful energy and certainty, a willingness to challenge convention and break the rules within limits. It was evolution, not revolution.

It was a promise short-lived. It ended with the explosion of gunfire and a brutal murder just short of a highway underpass in Dallas. In our collective shock that weekend, we knew something was terribly wrong. We experienced a common vulnerability, but we did not yet understand that the violence of a presidential assassination was a harbinger of much more violence to come in our lives at so many levels. I still have LIFE's special edition on the assassination and funeral. When I look at it now, I understand as I did not then that little John-John's salute was not just a farewell to his father; it also marked the passing of our post–World War II innocence.

Shortly we were a nation in a brawl with the conventions of our culture. Some of the battles were honorable and attacked wrongs long overdue to be corrected. Civil rights protests, especially in the South, and the uprisings of the inner cities forced white America to confront the magnitude of its racial hypocrisy. This racial passage in America was a violent gauntlet. "Bull" Connor and his attack dogs in Birmingham. Violence so bold a photograph in LIFE included a wounded James Meredith looking at his assailant in the bushes.

And the violence in the dark of night or out of sight of cameras. Black youngsters were pulled from school buses by stone-hard rednecks; homes were burned; civil rights workers were murdered.

In the big cities of the North and West, the order of battle changed. Irregular black armies, fueled by police and economic injustice, "burned, baby, burned" and shot back. Inner cities became combat zones. Reverse racism found a following. Black messiahs preached the politics of one color: black. Black-power gangs marauded through the sixties firing off rounds of menacing revolutionary rhetoric.

No act of violence during the sixties was more devastating to our national psyche than the burst of gunfire that stilled the voice of Martin Luther King, Jr. We don't have to await the long pull of history to judge the vision, courage, and influence of this man on his time. Moreover, what he set in motion continues. He forced white America to face its racism by inspiring black America to rise up, speak out, and fight back. It is a great legacy of the sixties, this beginning of the civil rights movement, but it is also a curse on the decade that it will be measured as well by the murder of Dr. King.

Simultaneously America was at war abroad and at war with itself about the war abroad. Vietnam. Again, violence. Violence on the battlefields, in the streets, on college campuses, within families. Violence to our traditions and institutions. Vietnam represented a monumental clash between the past and future. The morality of America's involvement in a war came into focus with an intensity never before experienced. Truly, however Vietnam is measured — militarily, politically, culturally, psychologically — this was a cosmic event. It changed the order of our universe.

The pain remains. It is etched in the elegant Vietnam Veterans Memorial: the names of 58,156 dead. It haunts those who survived one battlefield to encounter others in their minds when they returned. My guess is that there's also a pain of another kind in the memories of many war resisters. In their opposition to the war, how many were claiming the high ground of morality for purely selfish reasons? While they had access to the privilege of college deferments, good lawyers, friendly doctors, or alternative duty, other American families were sending their young sons off to those murderous jungles and getting them back in military caskets.

No war has ever received such distinguished and disturbing photo coverage, still and television. Week after week television, magazines, and newspapers delivered the anguish and frustration and death of Vietnam directly to our homes. In these pages you will see the award-winning work of courageous men who constantly risked death to photograph war as it is fought on the killing fields, not as it is portrayed in Hollywood or on recruiting posters. LIFE photographer Larry Burrows' pictures are particularly memorable; they make his own death in Vietnam all the more tragic.

Vietnam brought down one President and killed a senator who might have been — Lyndon Johnson and Robert F. Kennedy. There was a struggle that year for the soul of the Democratic party, with Eugene McCarthy standing slightly apart, in the role of catalyst and poet. On the other side, Richard Nixon. In my lifetime, presidential politics may never again be so charged with such profound choices, with such tumult and theater.

One night during the 1968 Democratic convention in Chicago, I was on riot duty for "NBC News" in front of the Hilton Hotel. There was a momentary lull in the battle, the two sides regrouping. As a credentialed reporter, I was able to walk through a space between the National Guard and police aligned on one side and thousands of protesters in rough formation on the other. I was struck by their common age—the young faces of the protesters and the equally young faces of the Guardsmen and police. America's future divided. Will this ever heal? I wondered. In 1968 there was reason to doubt whether it would.

The assassinations of national leaders, the crusade for civil rights, and the Vietnam War were the three great seismic events of the decade, but there were hundreds of aftershocks that taken together were at once unsettling, painful, and liberating.

Few institutions escaped some kind of structural change. Family, community, university, bank, church, law, the pillars of society were challenged to one degree or another. Nothing was beyond question for a child of the sixties, a generation unbounded by the limits of birth date. Dr. Spock in his sixties was as much a child of that time as was the barefoot girl in granny dress with daisies laced through her long, blond tresses.

Authority lost its privileged place almost overnight. Mothers, fathers, police, judges, teachers, the President of the United States—suddenly these authority figures were spending as much time defending their conduct as they were exercising their power. As with so much of what happened during the sixties, the assault on authority was uneven. Citizen coalitions rallied around common interests and forced politicians to abandon smoke-filled rooms. Consumers found a vibrant voice in the marketplace. Students forced the academies to listen as well as teach. Other challenges to authority were self-serving and mindless, exaggerated acts designed to replace one kind of authoritarian excess with another. Rigid, authoritarian conduct was no more attractive in ponytail and bell-bottoms than in pinstripes and button-down collar.

No institution underwent greater change during the sixties than the family. Ozzie and Harriet, David and Ricky were superficial, idealized symbols of the family of the fifties. The sixties made possible "All in the Family," with Archie, Edith, Mike, and Gloria. Theirs was not just some television contrivance. It broke through the artifice of Hollywood and caught the conflict underway in many families: parents hanging on to the old ways, while the kids mocked values and manners Mom and Dad never questioned.

There have been intergenerational feuds in families, I suppose, for as long as people have lived together as parent and child. What made those feuds so emotionally and psychologically painful during the sixties were the enormous gaps between the beliefs and conduct of so many parents and their children. Crew-cut World War II veterans looked up at the dinner table to see this stranger in shoulder-length hair, wearing one earring and blue jeans patched with pieces of the American flag, discussing the latest gimmick for escaping the draft. That the stranger was in fact a son only heightened the sense of betrayal and outrage. Mothers were lectured by daughters about their fealty to a life of mothering, cooking, and cleaning. Or daughters brought home boyfriends and announced they'd be sharing a bed for the weekend and please! no questions about marriage, it isn't that kind of a relationship.

Too many people gave up on the nuclear family, proclaiming it an anachronism, too confining for the easy mores of the moment. Divorce, just short of scandalous during the fifties, became routine in the sixties. So routine, couples understandably wondered, Why bother with marriage? Why not just live together until it no longer works and then split? For all the talk about commitment during the sixties, it was an elusive quality in the one relationship that demands it most, marriage. Yet, and this is another paradox of the time, when the familial fires of the sixties cooled and the rebuilding began, families took shape along new lines. Children of the sixties who became parents in the seventies and eighties weren't walled off from their children by wardrobe, music, ideas. Blue jeans, running shoes, long hair, rock and roll became common denominators instead of detonators. The sixties made it possible for parents to share the responsibility, to be free of the strictures of a narrowly cast mother or father role.

Women — whether mother, student, worker, manager — raised their consciousness and their voices in the sixties as they had at no other time in history. They knew they were not recognized and rewarded on the same scale as the least of men. They were beginning to ask why not? It was not a rhetorical question. It was backed by powerful political coalitions and the force of a moral argument that could not be swept aside by shibboleths from the past, including this one from Nietzsche, "It is dangerous to try equality with a woman... she will be rather content with subordination if the man is a man." Nietzsche plainly never met Gloria Steinem or, for that matter, Meredith Brokaw and millions of other women who not only are at ease with equality, but they understandably expect it. They also expect to make their own choices. More than twenty years after it made its way into the social contract, the clause defining the role of women remains a work in progress — but it will not be undone.

The sixties also brought us bean sprouts, brown rice, yogurt, whole grain breads, holistic medicine, and drugs. Let's get stoned! — but remember to eat our veggies. Widespread drug abuse today can be traced directly to the drug culture of the sixties. Looking back, what's astonishing is the casual, almost lighthearted approach to drug use then. The absence of foreboding. Someone said recently, "If you remember the sixties you weren't there." Drug use was a badge, certification of your place in the generation. In the fifties students learned to tap a keg of beer. In the sixties they smoked, dropped, and popped a wild array of renegade chemicals, hallucinogens, and narcotics. The fog of drugs hung over the decade like a poisonous cloud.

There were other highs, of course, not chemically induced. The decade began with Roger Maris and Mickey Mantle, but it became the time of the antihero in the popular culture, still another manifestation of the decade's determination to turn convention inside out. We went from balding Y. A. Tittle in his high-topped football shoes to shaggy Joe Namath, "Broadway Joe," and his brash guarantee that the upstart Jets would beat the Colts in the Super Bowl. Polite, soft-spoken Floyd Patterson gave way to Cassius Clay, who became Muhammad Ali, a supremely gifted fighter, maybe the best ever, an irresistible personality who taunted the Establishment much as he defeated his opponents in the ring, "floating like a butterfly, stinging like a bee." The Miracle Mets, written off as the laugh line of the national pastime, won the 1969 World Series. In sports, as in so much of life, the sixties refused to follow the script.

Not even in space. Our first astronauts — John Glenn, Alan Shepard, Walter Schirra, and the rest of the magnificent seven – were the kind of heroes we always celebrated: bold, brash, aw-shucks men who enjoyed the attention and took from it what they needed, discarding the rest. They were succeeded by the astronauts who made the quantum leap, the first men to walk on the moon – Neil Armstrong and Edwin "Buzz" Aldrin. Their place in history secure, they struggled with the demands of hero worship and finally gave up, each in his own way dropping out. One more American formula rewritten.

New forms were taking hold elsewhere on the popular front. Paul Newman and Robert Redford turned the Western toward previously unexplored territory in *Butch Cassidy and the Sundance Kid*. Warren Beatty and Faye Dunaway were vulnerable and touching as Bonnie and Clyde, updating the tough guy and his equally tough dame, Humphrey Bogart and Lauren Bacall. On stage *Hair* was more than a rock-and-roll musical. It was a theatrical portrait of the counterculture. The Troubadours, the Beatles, the Stones, the Grateful Dead, Jefferson Airplane, the Who, the Supremes, Dylan, Taylor, King, Baez, Simon & Garfunkel, Joplin, Hendrix – they, too, crashed through old barriers and created a new universe of music. And in this universe, a new form of popular religion flourished, the rock-and-roll church with its nocturnal, narcissistic, mischievous, antiauthoritarian creed financed by great gobs of cash eagerly offered up by faithful acolytes.

This was not a decade confined to American shores. Politically, Europe was under siege from the left. Its cultural and social institutions experienced traumas as great as those in the United States. Although we didn't realize it at the time, Chairman Mao ordered up the cultural revolution in mid-decade.

Still, for all the thunder and lightning, for all the fireworks, for all the tremors and proclamations of a new age, Richard Nixon was twice elected President by running against these changes and their prophets. Ironically, in Watergate he failed to understand that some of the changes did take hold, that the sixties were the beginning of the end of the imperial presidency. Watergate, however, did not invalidate the fact that a majority of the American voters were turned off, not turned on, by the sixties. Remember: this was also the decade of the Brady bunch and Mary Tyler Moore. In the sixties the Osmond family enjoyed its greatest success, and American flag lapel pins were the insignia of those who chose not to hear what was blowin' in the wind. Both Ron Ziegler and Elvis Presley were selected by the National Junior Chamber of Commerce as among the outstanding young men in America.

Future historians have a daunting task, making sense of the sixties. Some of the judgments are in, but they may not hold. Too much of what began then remains unresolved. For example, a friend who lost part of a leg and won the congressional Medal of Honor in Vietnam resists the idea of putting that war behind us. He argues we still have lessons to learn from it. We still have veterans for whom that war remains a nightmare without end. Civil rights is an unfinished agenda. New Wave music cannot drain the life from rock and roll. Assassination of national leaders gave way seamlessly to terrorism against innocent bystanders.

The exceptional photographs in this volume will remind you why, to one degree or another, the sixties were the time of our lives.

TOM BROKAW
*March 1989*

# LIFE THE '60S

# LIFE: The '60s

## *Civil Rights*

It is almost impossible, in the United States of today, to imagine the raw courage it took in the early 1960s, if you were a black person in the South, to sit down at a department store lunch counter, to stand in line to register to vote, to approach the front door of a school to enroll as a student, to dare sit in the front of a bus. Such privileges, and many others just as commonplace, were reserved for whites only.

Subtler forms of discrimination existed elsewhere, throughout American life. If evidence of black resentment were needed, riots in the Watts section of Los Angeles in 1965 killed thirty-four people and cost $40 million in property damage; in Newark in 1967 killed twenty-six and injured fifteen hundred; in Detroit, also in 1967, killed forty, injured more than a thousand, and took forty-seven hundred U.S. paratroopers and eight thousand National Guardsmen to quell.

It was possible in many parts of the U.S.—but especially in the South, which began within sight of the Washington Monument—to grow up in an all-white, or an all-black, community and catch sight of the other race only distantly. The accepted idea, the "way of life," was that blacks and whites lived in separate worlds, and according to the myth, those worlds were equal. Reality, however, was that blacks were mopping the hallways of the courthouse or carting away the garbage. Whites ran things.

But as the sixties dawned, stirrings of rebellion, of a desire for change, that had lain deep, fired by centuries of lynchings and rapes and myriad subtler wrongs and deprivations, blossomed at last into a civil revolution. The Supreme Court, in an epochal decision, in 1954 had ruled in the case of *Brown v. Board of Education of Topeka* that so-called separate but equal public schools in the U.S. were illegal. School boards, the court decreed, must "with all deliberate speed" begin to desegregate. Thus, by 1960, a generation of high school kids who had grown up acutely aware that in America apartheid was wrong, was entering college.

At that very same time, John F. Kennedy took office as President, with the promises he made during the campaign still ringing—that he would take steps to enact a broad new set of civil rights laws and that he would exercise "moral and persuasive leadership" to enforce the 1954 Supreme Court decision. No President in recent history had spoken so directly and so encouragingly to blacks and their sympathizers before. Moreover, the President's brother, Robert F. Kennedy, was in the office of U.S. attorney general, to see that those wishes were carried out. An atmosphere of protection for activism was clearly suggested, if not guaranteed.

The movement, as those engaged in civil rights work called their informal coalitions, gathered momentum and began challenging the official barriers to blacks seeking public accommodations. College students staged a sit-in demonstration: four young black men dared to sit down at a Woolworth's counter in Greensboro, North Carolina. The notion spread like wildfire, and groups such as the Student Non-violent Coordinating Committee (SNCC) and the Congress of Racial Equality (CORE) emerged to join—and to rival—old-line conservative black organizations such as the National Association for the Advancement of Colored People (NAACP) and the Urban League in the battle for equality. Many whites, too, turned out to join the sit-ins and the picket lines, to walk in the marches.

The arrival of the movement charged the atmosphere of life in the South as no event had done since the onset of the Civil War. The Ku Klux Klan and the National States Rights party and the American Nazi party fought blacks in the streets—often aided by obliging white sheriffs and local police. White Citizens' Councils set up "private" schools to accommodate students fleeing the threat of integrated schools. Meanwhile, state legislators in such capitals of resistance as Richmond and Montgomery spent whole sessions spinning theories of states' rights and "interposition" in an effort to squirm away from having to abide by the "Yankee court" edict.

But the conflict forged strong alliances among the nation's blacks, producing sturdy leaders. One major institution that flourished despite segregation throughout the South was the church. Many local civil rights leaders were ministers. One was Martin Luther King, Jr., newly arrived in Montgomery when forty-two-year-old Rosa Parks refused to surrender her bus seat to a white passenger on December 1, 1955. King, then twenty-six, assumed leadership of the bus boycott that ensued when Montgomery blacks supported Parks.

King's leadership, tested and developed through the boycott and other crises of the 1950s, was ready when the movement began to thrust its assault into other areas of discrimination. As blacks pressed harder against the color barriers, the segregationists fought back with fire hoses and police dogs, with bullets and explosives. Within days of King's historic "I Have a Dream" speech at the Lincoln Memorial in August of 1963, given on the occasion of the movement's March on Washington, four little girls were killed and another partially blinded by a bomb in a Birmingham Sunday school.

The South had erupted into a battleground, one on which often only the force of the federal troops or the presence of federal agents could prevail against the outraged segregationist locals. Just as it took federal officers to desegregate the schools in Little Rock in 1957, it required sixteen thousand federal troops to bring calm to the University of Mississippi when James Meredith, a black, tried to enroll in 1962. Similarly, only FBI men managed to solve the murder—by local white lawmen—of three civil rights workers near Philadelphia, Mississippi, in 1964.

But terrible as it often was, the violence and the concurrent news attention evoked by the nonviolent demonstrators won the effect sought by King and other leaders, arousing the conscience of the nation. In 1964 Congress enacted a broad-scale array of civil rights laws. Its major goal—equality in law—seemingly achieved, the movement thus gradually faded out of the headlines.

Today, many of the sixties' leaders of the movement, such as the Reverend Jesse Jackson, Andrew Young, Julian Bond, and others continue to work in politics, government, and the private sector, carrying on the old struggle to achieve black equality in full reality, full participation in the American dream.

Atlanta, Georgia, police took Dr. Martin Luther King, Jr. –
who had assumed leadership of the Montgomery bus boycott
and of the burgeoning civil rights movement – to court in
handcuffs for participating in a sit-in demonstration at a
lunch counter in the city's leading department store. Fifty-two
other demonstrators were released, but King was sentenced to
four months of hard labor. King was released on bail pending
appeal only after Democratic candidate John F. Kennedy
telephoned King's anxious wife, Coretta, and Kennedy's
brother Bobby phoned the judge.
1960, Don Uhrbrock >

A Montgomery, Alabama, woman walks to
support the 1956 boycott headed by Martin
Luther King, Jr., protesting segregation on
city buses. The historic boycott lasted more
than a year, until the U.S. Supreme Court
struck down the Jim Crow laws that made
blacks sit in back. The success of this boycott
is widely regarded as the birth of the civil
rights movement.
1956, Don Cravens

At his funeral, Mack Charles Parker's friends
and family mourn. A lynch mob dragged
Parker, twenty-three, from his jail cell in
Poplarville, Mississippi, and shot him after
a pregnant white woman told police she
wasn't sure, but she thought he was the man
who had raped her.
1959, Don Cravens

A Freedom Riders' bus, hit by a firebomb
thrown by whites, burns in Alabama. But the
rides, mounted to attack segregation from
Washington to New Orleans, continued.
1961, Joe Postiglione for *The Anniston Star*

Bayonets fixed, federal troops advance down an Oxford,
Mississippi, street to arrest Major General Edwin A. Walker
on charges of insurrection. Walker led rioters protesting
admission of James Meredith, twenty-nine, a black, to the
University of Mississippi.
1962, Lynn Pelham from Rapho Guillamette >

Birmingham, Alabama, was probably the most harshly
segregated large city in the U.S. Early in 1963 the city became
the target for wide-scale, nonviolent black demonstrations
against such conditions. Thousands of protesters were arrested
until the jails were full, but the demonstrations continued.
Police Commissioner Eugene "Bull" Connor, who became the
symbol of police brutality, ordered that high-velocity fire
hoses be turned on the demonstrators.
1963, Charles Moore from Black Star >

*Water from fire hoses pins Birmingham protesters to the walls of a building. Scenes like this occurred daily as Birmingham demonstrators pressed demands for access to snack bars and stores, nonracial hiring, and a biracial committee to work on yet more desegregation.*
1963, Charles Moore from Black Star

*Glaring at the firemen who have just assaulted him with a water hose, a Birmingham black gives expression to his bitterness.*
< 1963, Charles Moore from Black Star

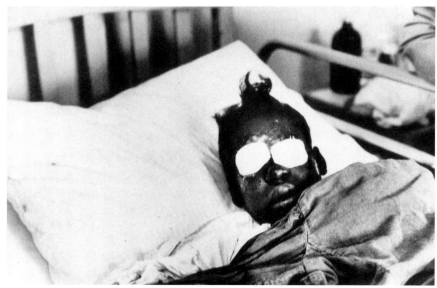

*Demonstrators are set upon in Birmingham by attack dogs under the control of trained handlers. The dogs tore the flesh and clothing of the protesters. The viciousness of this brutality brought expressions of support from all over the world for Birmingham blacks.*
< 1963, Charles Moore from Black Star

*Sarah Jean Collins, twelve, lies nearly blinded in a Birmingham hospital. As Sarah's Sunday school class was ending, a bomb exploded in the basement of her church, killing her sister and three other small girls and leaving Sarah blinded in one eye.*
< 1963, Frank Dandridge

*Gloria H. Richardson, a civil rights leader in Cambridge, Maryland, responds to an order from a National Guardsman enforcing martial law.*
1963, Fred Ward

Andrew Goodman (arrow), twenty, in training for civil rights work, linked arms with others to sing the freedom song "We Shall Overcome." Goodman also heard warnings of the dangers he would face doing voter registration work in Mississippi during the summer. In 1964, outside Philadelphia, Mississippi, the worst came true: Goodman; another white, Michael Schwerner, twenty-four; and James Chaney, twenty-one, a local black, were brutally murdered with the cooperation of the Ku Klux Klan and the local police. The tragic killings were the subject of a book, Three Lives for Mississippi, by William Bradford Huie, and of a 1989 film, Mississippi Burning.
1964, Steve Schapiro

At first this charred wreckage of their station wagon – deep in Bogue Chito swamp in Mississippi – was the only trace to be found of the three missing civil rights workers as one of the most infamous atrocities of the decade came to light. Then President Lyndon Johnson ordered FBI agents, a detachment of navy men, and a former CIA director onto the case. Local rednecks sniggered confidently as the swamp was combed – but the bodies of Schwerner, Goodman, and Chaney were eventually located and exhumed from an earthen dam.
1964, Steve Schapiro >

Sheriff Lawrence Rainey (right) showed his nonchalance at being charged with the murders of the three young civil rights workers by chewing tobacco during the arraignment. Rainey was later acquitted, but Deputy Cecil Price (left) and six others were convicted and jailed.
1964, Bill Reed >

13

*Protesting police violence during voter registration campaigns, marchers trudged from Selma, Alabama, to Montgomery. But police turned the six hundred marchers back with gas and truncheons. Finally President Lyndon Johnson ordered an Alabama National Guard escort, and the marchers – their numbers swelled to twenty-five thousand by supporters from around the U.S. – arrived in the state capital.*
*1965, Steve Schapiro*

Black Muslim leader Malcolm X, shaded by an umbrella on a hot June day, urges a Harlem crowd to "get the white monkey off your backs." Two years later, black assassins shot him to death on a Manhattan stage.
< 1963, Ted Russell

James Meredith, who desegregated the University of Mississippi in 1962, was shot from ambush while on a 220-mile march from Memphis, Tennessee, to Jackson, Mississippi, to encourage blacks to register and vote. As Meredith fell, he turned to look at his assailant (in the undergrowth to the left). This photograph won a Pulitzer Prize.
< 1966, Associated Press

Mourners say farewell to Medgar Evers, slain Mississippi civil rights leader, at his funeral in Jackson.
1963, John Loengard

At the funeral of murdered Mississippi civil rights worker
Medgar Evers, his widow, Myrlie, comforts their son. Evers,
thirty-seven, NAACP field secretary, was shot in the back by
an assassin hiding with a rifle in a honeysuckle thicket across
the street from his home in Jackson as he returned from a
meeting. The murder occurred just hours after President Kennedy made a historic national TV address calling civil rights
a moral issue.
1963, John Loengard

A persistent reporter interviews a Congress of Racial Equality
(CORE) demonstrator protesting job discrimination as police
drag him away at the opening of the New York World's Fair.
1964, Gordon Tenney

More than two hundred thousand people
pack the lawn around the Reflecting Pool in
front of the Lincoln Memorial to hear Martin
Luther King, Jr., speak on August 28, 1963,
at the largest civil rights demonstration
in U.S. history. "I have a dream," King declared, "that my four little children will one
day live in a nation where they will not be
judged by the color of their skin but by the
content of their character . . . when all of God's
children, black men and white men, Jews
and Gentiles, Protestants and Catholics, will
be able to join hands and sing, in the words
of the old Negro spiritual, 'Free at last! Free
at last! Thank God Almighty, we are free
at last!'"
1963, Paul Schutzer >

*Children cautiously cross a street in Watts.
"Blood" on the wall of the grocery behind
them identified the store as black-owned,
protecting it during 1965 riots.*
1966, Bill Ray

*Hatred and rage burst into flaming riots that
roared through Watts, a black ghetto of Los
Angeles, for six days in August 1965, killing
thirty-four and causing $40 million worth of
property damage. Here firemen battle one
of the spreading fires that were nearly
impossible to contain.*
<< 1965, Co Rentmeester

22

*A Newark cop checks Joe Bass, Jr., twelve, wounded by police shotgun blast during riots.*
1967, Bud Lee

*Johannesburg policeman uses his cane as a whip to drive a black spectator from the courthouse. It was the opening day of the trial of 130 South African black women who had been arrested for protesting a new regulation requiring them to carry ID passes.*
1958, Barry Von Below for
*The Johannesburg Star*

*Police in Sharpeville, near Johannesburg, South Africa, killed fifty-six people when they fired into a crowd of blacks demonstrating against tightened racial laws. Some in the gathering had laughed when the shooting started, thinking the police were using blanks. Police continued firing even when people ran.*
1960, Warwick Robinson

*At rebel headquarters in Algiers, defiant French settlers sing
the "Marseillaise" after hearing President Charles de Gaulle's
radio broadcast urging them to accept self-determination
for Algiers and end war.*
1960, Loomis Dean

自由民主党 [...]

日本社会党 石稲次郎氏

民主社会党 西尾末広氏

Already mortally wounded, Inejiro
Asanuma, chairman of Japan's Socialist
party, pleads for protection from his assassin,
a political fanatic who leapt on stage with a
sword before a stunned audience of three
thousand.
1960, Yasushi Nagao for Mainichi Shimbun

England's Queen Elizabeth II takes a half-mile ride through
India's royal palace grounds on her first visit to the former
colony, timed to mark the thirteenth anniversary of its birth
as a republic.
1961, Hank Walker >

High on an escarpment in the Himalayas, Indian soldiers struggle to help a truck up a steep primitive road during the battle with China over the border.
1962, Larry Burrows

This is a photograph of the photograph of captured U.S. pilot Gary Powers that was exhibited by the Russians after his U-2 spy plane crashed on Soviet territory. The incident wrecked the long-awaited Paris summit between President Dwight D. Eisenhower and Soviet premier Nikita Khrushchev and, LIFE reported, "threatened to put the cold war in its deepest freeze since Stalin died."
1960, Carl Mydans

In Paris for the aborted summit on disarmament, Khrushchev denounced the U.S. for sending reconnaissance flights over Russia. "I was horrified to learn that the President had endorsed those aggressive acts," Khrushchev said. Ike said spying was "a distasteful but vital necessity."
1960, Carl Mydans >

An East Berlin border guard leaps across the barbed wire into West Berlin – and freedom. In August 1961, work on the permanent concrete wall had just begun. After this escape, officers kept guards well behind the wire barriers to thwart any other attempts.
1961, Associated Press

West Germans fashioned a memorial to two who were shot while attempting to swim the Spree River in a desperate flight from East Berlin. A picture of one is shown at the base of the cross with the words, "You could have been our brother." The other victim is memorialized by the rough stone on which is carved, "To the Unknown Refugee."
1962, Walter Sanders

East German soldiers (in mushroom helmets) and police hurriedly remove the body of Peter Fechtin, slain while trying to escape East Berlin. Fechtin lay screaming for help for more than an hour before dying. Afterward, West Berliners stoned a Soviet bus and jeered U.S. troops for not rescuing him.
1962, Bild Zeitung >

*Near the end of his successful two-year campaign to over-throw Cuba's Batista government, Fidel Castro speaks with a reporter as he rests at his headquarters in the hills.*
1958, Andrew St. George

*Relations between the U.S. and Cuba became so strained that President Eisenhower severed diplomatic ties and ordered the American staff home. Here, their luggage is tied down aboard a truck outside the U.S. embassy in Havana.*
1961, Paul Schutzer

*A priest looks for help for a Venezuelan soldier wounded during bitter fighting with rebel marines in Puerto Cabello. The two-day battle, which killed four hundred and wounded one thousand, ended when machete-wielding peasants helped oust rebels.*
1962, Hector Rondon

This finance company billboard ironically states the plight of
Johnstown, Pennsylvania, where 16.9 percent of steelworkers
were unemployed in the early sixties.
1961, Paul Schutzer

During the Democratic primary campaign, John F. Kennedy
talks about economic conditions with West Virginia coal miners. Cool at first to this rich Easterner, the miners warmed up
as Kennedy showed he understood their problems. His victory
here in a largely Protestant state showed his Catholicism
would not be a major problem elsewhere in the election.
1960, Hank Walker >

*Pandemonium breaks out on the floor of the Democratic con-*
*vention as delegates hear John F. Kennedy's name placed*
*in nomination by Minnesota governor Orville L. Freeman.*
*Kennedy quickly piled up 806 votes to Lyndon B. Johnson's*
*409, and the convention voted to make it unanimous.*
1960, Ralph Crane

*This was John F. Kennedy's favorite photograph of himself. One of his greatest pleasures was walking the dunes near his family's home at Hyannis Port, Massachusetts.*
1959, Mark Shaw

*Instantly recognizable even in silhouette, the brothers Kennedy — Jack, forty-three, left, and Bobby, thirty-four, his campaign manager — confer in a Los Angeles hotel room on the eve of Jack's nomination as Democratic candidate for President of the United States.*
1960, Hank Walker >

*As a reporter stretches a mike to catch their words, Vice President–Elect Lyndon Baines Johnson doffs his cowboy hat to welcome his running mate to the LBJ ranch, their first meeting since winning the White House.*
1960, Paul Schutzer

*While campaigning for president, John F. Kennedy repeatedly hammered his theme: to get America "moving again."*
1960, Paul Schutzer

President Eisenhower, stung by Kennedy's campaign asser-
tions that the nation was standing still, spoke in Philadelphia
before a huge portrait of Nixon, plugged the GOP ticket, and
defended his administration. "Never have Americans achieved
so much in so short a time," he said of his eight years.
1960, Walter Sanders


High points in the presidential election campaign were 4 one-
hour TV debates between John F. Kennedy (left) and Richard
M. Nixon. Kennedy was the underdog as the debates began,
but with his self-assured manner and grasp of the facts, he
emerged from the series with a slight edge over Nixon and
maintained it through the election.
1960, Paul Schutzer >>

# LIFE: The '60s

## The Kennedy Years

He is forever there in the national album of shared memories: a man for whom the word *charisma* might have been coined. Taking the oath of his high office in Washington that freezing inauguration day in 1961, John F. Kennedy declared, "We shall pay any price, bear any burden, meet any hardship, support any friend, oppose any foe, to assure the survival and the success of liberty." It was an audacious assertion, tough rhetoric that had real punch mainly because the handsome young President was infusing it with his own enthusiasm and spirit. He was, he said in his ringing voice, one of "a new generation of Americans—born in this century, tempered by war, disciplined by a hard and bitter peace."

But much more of the Kennedy era lingers than just the bittersweet keepsakes of memory. Jack Kennedy worked tangible changes in American life—mainly in the area of civil rights and equal opportunity—and in how Americans think about politics and politicians, what they expect from their government. This youngest President ever elected ran on a promise to "get America moving again." His campaign platform was a virtual agenda of the major societal tasks confronting our time, pledging him to work for stronger civil rights protections, increased defense spending, arms control, aid to underdeveloped countries, old-age medical help, cancer research, disability insurance, conservation of natural resources, environmental and consumer protections, slum clearance, an accelerated space program. Kennedy labeled his administration forever when he declared, as he accepted his party's nomination, "We stand today on the edge of a New Frontier—the frontier of the 1960s."

The public relished the daily Kennedy drama, eagerly watching as Kennedy, who called himself an idealist without illusions, grappled with the problems of his era with characteristic shirt-sleeved, one-on-one directness. When Martin Luther King, Jr., was jailed during the very height of the presidential campaign, Kennedy himself called Mrs. King to sympathize—despite the possible cost of such a call in terms of the votes in the conservative white South. To demonstrate his concern as President for underdeveloped countries, Kennedy set up the Peace Corps, and in the twenty years after he established the seemingly quixotic agency, no fewer than eighty-five thousand Americans volunteered to help. When steel magnates hiked prices, Kennedy himself forced them to roll back the increase by publicly condemning their greed.

Internationally, too, his style was personal, forthright. Sometimes, as in the abortive invasion of Cuba and, perhaps, in sending American soldiers to Vietnam as "advisers," his moves were mistakes. But when he ignored his military counselors' urgings of war over the Cuban missile crisis and opted for diplomacy and blockades instead, Kennedy may have averted World War III. Just as his support buoyed American blacks, he offered comradeship to Germans, who heard him declare at the Berlin Wall, "Ich bin ein Berliner." And he coolly proceeded, despite Russian aggression in Berlin and Cuba, to forge an historic agreement with the Soviets banning atmospheric nuclear tests.

John F. Kennedy was the first of the modern, high-visibility, video-era Presidents—the first to hold live press conferences on radio and TV—and the first of a brand-new breed of hard-nosed, hardball, media-savvy politicians. Behind that hatless, jaunty figure of Jack

Kennedy on the campaign trail in 1960 was a whole battalion of relatives and longtime allies—led by brother Bobby—who were doing the detail work. Many of these look-alike members of what came to be known as Kennedy's Irish Mafia moved with him into the White House. His brother Bobby became attorney general; brother-in-law Sargent Shriver was director of the Peace Corps.

But Jack Kennedy was more than just a figurehead. He was a genuine war hero, a congressman from 1947 to 1953, a two-term U.S. senator, and a Pulitzer Prize–winning author. In several ways Kennedy's career was a triumph over adversity—the loss of a beloved and idolized older brother, Joe, Jr., in World War II; severe childhood illnesses; and a crippled back so painful he almost died from surgery to correct it. This handsome millionaire Harvard man became the beloved hero of millions of ordinary Americans because he was the embodiment of their dreams. Jack Kennedy was the inheritor of what looked, for a while, as if it were going to be the happiest of endings to a real life fairy tale version of the American dream.

The incredible saga of the Kennedy family began in 1848, when a Kennedy fled the potato famine that was ravaging Ireland to come to Boston, and climaxed 112 years later, when his great-grandson moved into the White House. He wanted to be there, Jack Kennedy said bluntly, because "that's where the power is." And once he arrived, the Kennedys imprinted their style on every aspect of American life. Women everywhere tried to dress like Kennedy's beautiful wife, Jackie. The public warmed to Jackie as to no first lady in modern memory, admiring her chic clothes, envying her deft touch at transforming fusty old 1600 Pennsylvania Avenue into a glowing candle-lit salon wherein the likes of Pablo Casals—and his cello—were guests. Former photographer for the *Washington Times-Herald*, equestrienne, a Sorbonne-educated debutante who could charm the most jaded official Washingtonians with such imaginative fetes as holding a state dinner at Mount Vernon, George Washington's mansion on the Potomac, Jackie was a breathtaking new kind of first lady.

Americans could not seem to get enough of seeing the Kennedys, their irrepressible children, the family frolics on the beach at Hyannis Port, the weekend touch football games, and the long hikes—ordered by the President to restore the vigor (pronounced "vigah" in this Boston-Irish administration) of the staff exhausted after a week of sixteen-hour days toiling on the New Frontier. Life on the New Frontier was heady, exciting drama, and the whole nation was caught up in it.

And then on a sunny November day, now etched indelibly with horror and grief in the national memory, before a cheering crowd that lined the parade route in Dallas, the assassin fired his rifle with deadly aim and murdered the President, and with him died a part of the American dream.

The day after he was elected President, a jubilant John F. Kennedy stood with his family at their home in Hyannis Port, Massachusetts. From left: Ethel (Mrs. Robert) Kennedy; Stephen Smith; Eunice (Mrs. Sargent) Shriver; Jean (Mrs. Stephen) Smith; Rose (Mrs. Joseph) Kennedy; Joseph P. Kennedy; the President; Robert F. Kennedy; Jacqueline (Mrs. John) Kennedy; Patricia (Mrs. Peter) Lawford; Edward Kennedy; Sargent Shriver; Joan (Mrs. Edward) Kennedy; Peter Lawford.
1960, Paul Schutzer

The bitter strain of a narrow – less than two-tenths of 1 percent – defeat etched in their faces, Pat and Richard Nixon thank campaign workers at the Los Angeles hotel where they waited for election returns. A standing ovation brought Pat to the verge of tears.
1960, Hank Walker

At an inauguration day ball with his wife, Jacqueline, John F. Kennedy exudes all the confidence and decisiveness that supercharged his campaign. In his address a few hours earlier, Kennedy had said, "Let the word go forth from this time and place, to friend and foe alike, that the torch has been passed to a new generation of Americans."
1961, Paul Schutzer >

Cellist Pablo Casals bows to applause at a concert the
Kennedys held to honor Governor Muñoz Marin of Puerto
Rico and his wife. Casals had last played at the White House
for President Theodore Roosevelt, in 1904.
1961, Mark Shaw

Young ladies in white gloves listen attentively to poet Robert
Frost at a White House dinner honoring leaders in the fields
of literature, science, and peace, including forty-nine Nobel
Prize winners. Addressing his guests, President Kennedy said,
"I think this is the most extraordinary collection of talent, of
human knowledge . . . ever gathered . . . at the White House, with
the possible exception of when Thomas Jefferson dined alone."
1962, Arthur Rickerby >

*Cuban soldiers, carbines at the ready, escort captive Cuban exiles who surrendered during the abortive Bay of Pigs invasion.*
1961 (no credit)

*President John F. Kennedy and his predecessor, Dwight Eisenhower, met at Camp David to demonstrate national unity in the wake of the Bay of Pigs fiasco. Castro stopped the invasion within seventy-two hours.*
1961, Edward Clark

*Robert F. Kennedy, thirty-six, attorney general of the United States, sips coffee in his office. LIFE called Bobby a "hard-headed, hard-driving kid brother, Capital's No. 2 man."*
1962, Edward Clark >

*The United States destroyer* Vesole *(bottom) stalks a Soviet freighter, the* Polzunov, *and monitors the Russian withdrawal of nuclear missiles from Cuba. In October of 1962, reconnaissance photos revealed Russian bases equipped with forty missiles with atomic warheads aimed at the U.S., others under construction, and twenty-five ships en route with yet more missiles. Kennedy surprised and impressed the Russians by ordering a naval blockade and delivering a blunt ultimatum to Khrushchev: remove the bases, get the missiles out, and turn the freighters around. By promising there would be no U.S. invasion of Cuba, JFK diplomatically provided Khrushchev with a face-saving way to accept. After six tense days, with the world holding its breath, Khrushchev backed down and agreed to the terms, ending one of the most dangerous crises of the decade.*
1962, Carl Mydans

The photographer captioned this portrait, which he took while on special assignment for LIFE: "Fidel's partner in running Cuba is Ernesto 'Che' Guevara, an impetuous man with burning eyes and profound intelligence who seems born to make revolution—if it hadn't been in Cuba, it would have been somewhere else."
1963, Henri Cartier-Bresson

The welcoming embrace between a Liberian teacher and an American Peace Corps teacher illustrates the feeling and dedication that characterized the Peace Corps movement. John F. Kennedy proposed the Corps during his 1960 presidential campaign and established it on March 1, 1961, two months after his inauguration. Thousands of Americans were inspired to give their time and effort in overseas service with the Peace Corps.
1964, Pierre Boulat from Cosmos

Richard Burton and Julie Andrews starred in the Kennedys' favorite musical, the Alan Lerner–Frederick Loewe–Moss Hart smash hit, Camelot, the story of King Arthur and Guinevere—and her lover, Sir Lancelot.
1960, Milton H. Greene >

University of Southern California's Delta Chi shows the form that won a forty-two-mile hospital-bed race from the California state line to downtown Las Vegas. After LIFE reported the fad was sweeping Canadian colleges, a Hollywood publicity man set up this race to promote a rental agency and a Las Vegas motel.
1961, Bill Bridges

*Pepe Sapronetti, Las Vegas hairdresser, works on his fast-draw style in front of the mirrors in his salon, striving for the thirty-five hundredths of a second necessary to compete in national six-gun competitions.*
1961, J. R. Eyerman

*Larry Shaw, a Malibu teenager, lives the life thousands of young Californians feel is the only one worth living – that of a surfer.*
< 1961, Allan Grant

Couples dance the twist: sheer sensual, frenetic motion, and no touching. Black singer Hank Ballard wrote and choreographed the song, and Chubby Checker's recording had the whole world doing it, young and old, rich and poor. The New York Safety Council reported forty-nine cases of twisted backs, but, said Chubby, "The twist is big because it's so swingy – and oh, so easy."
1961, Ted Russell

Barbara Hernandez, nineteen, quaffs a cola while checking the chalkboard against the tape for a St. Louis brokerage during the market's historic 34.95-point plunge on May 28, 1962, the sharpest drop since the 1929 crash.
1962, Herb Weitman >

60

*Racks of new dresses can loom up suddenly on a sidewalk in New York's Seventh Avenue garment district.*
< 1960, Walter Sanders

*Norman Norell, preeminent American fashion designer, is surrounded by models wearing the styles of the twenties from his 1960 collection. Their eye makeup is copied from the Kees Van Dongen painting of the period, on the wall behind them.*
< 1960, Milton H. Greene

*A model at designer Pierre Cardin's 1962 Paris showing wears Cardin's chiffon hat with matching blouse and loosely draped stole.*
1962, Paul Schutzer

The sixties introduced many fashion innovations, none
viewed with more alarm than the topless bathing suit. While
it enlivened the summer of 1964, it was not around by the
summer of 1965.
1964, Henry Grossman

LIFE plunged right into the topless swimsuit story, reporting
primly that designer Rudi Gernreich's gag outfit "was actu-
ally being bought by hundreds of women — and even worn in
public by a brazen few." The magazine gave one of them this
fishy stare.
1964, Paul Schutzer

*A tourist at Fort Sumter in the harbor of Charleston, South Carolina, takes a keen interest in a Civil War cannon.*
1960, Alfred Eisenstaedt

*Although this American dessert originated Down East, deep-dish blueberry pie is now enjoyed from sea to shining sea.*
1967, Fred Lyon

One of the world's greatest ballerinas, Galina Ulanova takes a bow at fifty-two. Said writer Aleksey Tolstoy, after watching Ulanova dance, "I don't know why you're so excited. After all, she's just an ordinary goddess."
1962, Albert Kahn

American dancer Katherine Dunham shook up the natives with an impromptu performance in Dakar. She was there on a fifteen-thousand-mile search for authentic Senegalese dances, musicians, and costumes for her new show, Bamboche.
1962, Terence Spencer

*Spy novelist Ian Fleming stands in front of a rare 4¹/₂-liter Bentley – with an Amhurst-Villier supercharger just above the license plate – just like the one James Bond, 007, himself drove in* Moonraker.
1962, Loomis Dean

*Jazz clarinetist Benny Goodman gives Moscow fans a sweet toot while on tour in Russia.*
1962, Stan Wayman

*A couple enjoy a noontime respite beside the Seine in Paris.*
1963, Alfred Eisenstaedt >

John F. Kennedy, with Jacqueline and
daughter Caroline, at his home in Hyannis
Port, Massachusetts.
1959, Mark Shaw

John F. Kennedy was in Dallas with his wife on Friday, November 22, 1963, to give a fund-raising speech at noon. The sun was intense that day, and the crowds were large and enthusiastic. A Dallas clothing manufacturer, Abraham Zapruder, had chosen a spot on a slight rise along the motorcade's route from which to take 8-mm home movies of the President as he passed. The eight seconds that the movie lasted were the same seconds in which Lee Harvey Oswald fired from the window of the Texas School Book Depository. In this frame, Kennedy has been hit in the throat by the first bullet, and Texas governor John Connally, in the middle seat, also has been hit. The fatal shot is about to strike the President.

1963, Abraham Zapruder

*The news of the assassination broke with stunning force. In New York, horror and disbelief distort a woman's face as she learns of President Kennedy's death.*

1963, Stan Wayman

Bound for Washington, D.C., aboard Air Force One *after the assassination, Vice President Lyndon Baines Johnson was sworn in as President. He is flanked by his wife, Lady Bird, on his right and Jacqueline Kennedy on his left.*
< 1963, Cecil W. Stoughton

*A photographer's glimpse of a rifle barrel in a sixth-floor window of the Texas School Book Depository during the assassination led to the quick arrest of Lee Harvey Oswald. As evidence mounted linking Oswald to the slaying of the President, police decided to move him to a maximum security jail. As Oswald was led through the basement at police head-quarters toward an armored car, nightclub owner Jack Ruby broke through the police guard and killed Oswald with one shot. The shooting was seen on live TV by millions who had hardly left their sets during the days in which the tragedy unfolded.*
1963, Jack Beers for *The Dallas Morning News*

*Following President Kennedy's coffin to St. Matthew's Cathedral in Washington, D.C., with Mrs. Kennedy are, from left: James Auchincloss, Jacqueline Kennedy's half brother; Mrs. Lyndon B. Johnson; Attorney General Robert Kennedy; Peace Corps director and Mrs. Kennedy's brother-in-law Sargent Shriver; Mrs. Kennedy's brother-in-law Stephen Smith; and Senator Edward Kennedy. Others are Secret Service agents.*
1963, © Henri Dauman

*At his father's funeral, John F. Kennedy, Jr., salutes as the*
*coffin is carried from the cathedral in Washington, D.C.*
1963, UPI/Bettmann Newsphotos

Georgia O'Keeffe sits beside the chimney on the roof of her
desert ranch in New Mexico. Much of the stark, purified land-
scape she could see from here – along with the desert's flow-
ers, bones, and clouds – found its way into her paintings with
a style that was uniquely her own. O'Keeffe first visited New
Mexico in 1929 and was increasingly identified with it until
her death, in 1986.
1968, John Loengard

For this portrait, Irish playwright Sean O'Casey – whose
humor and love of life filled plays such as Juno and the
Paycock, The Plough and the Stars, and Within the Gates –
put on a red robe made for him by his daughter Shivaun.
< 1964, Gjon Mili

*Konosuke Matsushita, Japan's most successful industrialist, publisher, and author, founded a philosophical institute in Kyoto that he visits several days a week so he can walk in its raked gravel garden and talk with young philosophers.*
1964, Bill Ray

*English poet and author Robert Graves stops to rest while on a walk in Manhattan.*
1963, © Bob Gomel >

*On an early autumn evening, cascades of water fall from the Maderna fountain in St. Peter's Square in Rome as people await the start of ceremonies marking the opening of the Second Vatican Council.*

< 1962, Paul Schutzer

*John XXIII, a wise and compassionate son of peasants, began his reign as pope in 1958. He is weary and ill in this portrait, made shortly before his death, in June 1963.*

1963, David Lees

*Dancer Rudolf Nureyev joined Britain's prima ballerina Margot Fonteyn to dance in* Swan Lake *with the Vienna Opera Ballet. Nureyev, who had defected from Russia in 1961, became friends with Fonteyn after she invited him to debut in England that year.*
< 1964, Lord Snowdon

*In Oxford, Mississippi, the real locale of his greatest novels, William Faulkner latches the door to his stable.*
1962, Martin J. Dain

*Jacques d'Amboise, at twenty-eight America's first great male ballet dancer, swings his children, Christopher, three (left), and George, six, on the shore of a lake in Washington State.*
1962, John Dominis

John Huston ponders an upcoming scene as
Cardinal Glennon in the movie version of
the 1950 best-seller The Cardinal. It was the
veteran director's first appearance in front
of the cameras since he had given himself a
role in Treasure of the Sierra Madre.
1963, Steve Schapiro

Swiss sculptor Alberto Giacometti with one
of his characteristically stylized heads.
1964, Loomis Dean

Self-exiled poet Ezra Pound rests in a giant
straw chair at his home in Venice, Italy. He
was once committed to a Washington, D.C.,
mental hospital after he was found unfit for
trial for treason after making pro-Fascist
radio broadcasts from Italy in the 1940s.
1963, David Lees >

Sir Winston Churchill flashes his trademark victory signal from his stretcher upon his arrival back in London after falling and breaking his thigh in Monte Carlo. Churchill, eighty-seven, medicated himself with brandy and cigars.
1962, Derek Bayes

After funeral services, Sir Winston Churchill's casket is carried from St. Paul's Cathedral by Grenadier Guards. To the left is former Prime Minister Harold Macmillan. The casket was shrouded with a Union Jack, on which rested a black velvet cushion bearing the diamond-and-gold insignia of the Order of the Garter.
1965, Dominique Berretty >

While Number 10 Downing Street, London, quarters of England's prime minister, is usually the scene of official comings and goings, it can also be the scene of informal carryings-on, too — such as this slightly flirtatious visit being paid by some nannies to the bobbies on duty.
1961, Phillip Jones Griffiths

Adlai Stevenson, former governor of Illinois and unsuccessful Democratic candidate for President in 1952 and 1956, was the generally unflappable U.S. ambassador to the United Nations from 1961 to 1965. He was the point man dealing publicly with the Soviets during the Cuban missile crisis.
1964, Steve Schapiro

President Dwight David Eisenhower lies in state in the rotunda of the U.S. Capitol.
1969, Bob Gomel >

A worker hoses mud off antique breastplates after devastating floods that wrecked a third of Italy's economy, ravaged thousands of acres of farmland – and imperiled Florence's priceless trove of art.
1966, David Lees

Israeli volunteers, who flew to Florence to help in the massive international art rescue mission, carry Matteo Rosselli's Christ and the Wife of Zebedee from a flooded church to the restoration room at the Uffizi Gallery.
1966, David Lees >

90

*Egyptians flatten themselves to the ground in surrender
to advancing Israeli troops in the Gaza Strip during the
Six-Day War in June 1967. The battle was precipitated by
Egypt's closure of the Strait of Tiran, threatening Israel's
access to the Red Sea.*
1967, David Rubinger

*An Israeli commander scans the battlefield during the
Six-Day War.*
< 1967, Denis Cameron from Pix

# LIFE: The '60s

## *Music*

Like troubadours who sang the news through the Dark Ages, musicians of the sixties spread the word of a dawning better America among the nation's youth. Their songs exulted in a mood of limitless hope, of militant resistance to war, and of expectant anticipation of a bright new day.

Just as the snap transition from relaxed, bald, grandfatherly Dwight Eisenhower to brisk, thatchy Jack Kennedy in the White House signaled a sea change in politics and governmental style, so did the very look of sixties musicians broadcast the news: "The times they are a-changin'." Pat Boone, Frank Sinatra, Bing Crosby were still around on the charts of course. But crowding them out of the center of the spotlight, drawing the mobs of shrieking teenyboppers in these heady new days, was a whole new kind of musical entertainer, the likes of which Tin Pan Alley, Nashville, and the rest of the world of mainstream music had never seen before.

The powerful beat and compelling lyrics of black music—barred on many white radio stations through the late fifties—began to penetrate white awareness, transforming popular music. Jazz had always been black. Now, rhythm and blues, the rotgut sax of Earl Bostic, the powerhouse vocals of Motown began to be heard—and copied. By the end of the decade, blacks would be at center stage, too, represented by superstars such as Jimi Hendrix and Aretha Franklin.

From the raucous clubs of Liverpool came the Beatles, electrifying viewers of Ed Sullivan's TV variety show just as Elvis had a decade before. Assaulted by the Beatles, who came along behind rock performers such as Chuck Berry and Jerry Lee Lewis, popular music began to be blasted loose forever from its ties to prosaic, old, real-world June-Moon-Spoon. They were just magically irresistible, and soon the country was humming melodies such as "I Want to Hold Your Hand" and "A Hard Day's Night."

Hair got longer, drugs appeared as never before, and soon the Beatles and other groups were singing directly to kids of a secret world only they knew about, of life in the Yellow Submarine, and Sgt. Pepper's Lonely Hearts Club Band, and Strawberry Fields Forever. It was theme music to a wonderful nonsense world of utter fantasy—which made all the sense in the world if you were young enough, and hip enough, to dig it.

In the wake of John and Paul and George and Ringo came a wacky battalion of kindred free spirits: the Rolling Stones, with wicked Mick Jagger bounding shirtless about the stage; the Grateful Dead; nutty groups such as Herman's Hermits, howling songs like "I'm Henry the VIII I Am."

Music had soared into a surreal, psychedelic stratosphere along with painting and the other arts—helped aloft by a dollop of marijuana and a wallop of post-thermonuclear angst. Lyrics often held hidden meanings. "Puff the Magic Dragon," for example, was a winsome fantasy song—and a bittersweet ballad about life assisted by marijuana. And "Lucy in the Sky With Diamonds" possibly alluded to LSD.

The surging power of song would help to change the world by the end of the sixties, drawing the young together, giving them courage and hope and laughter. From the coffeehouses of Cambridge, Massachusetts, and Berkeley came the sinuous thrum of Martin guitars; the clear, sweet soprano of Joan Baez; the urgent, nasal whine of Bob Dylan. Hearing them, nobody needed a weatherman to know which way the wind was blowin'. Dylan, Baez, and a host of comrades like Pete Seeger, Odetta, and Peter, Paul, and Mary became familiar figures at the protest rallies – about civil rights, the war in Vietnam, women's lib, gay rights, the environment – that constantly seemed to be in progress.

The reaction on the other side of the footlights was an electrified recognition, a hungry acceptance: here were performers who *knew* and who told it like it was – and who *lived* their art. Many, such as Hendrix, were casualties of drugs. Drawled Joplin, who died at twenty-seven from a heroin overdose, "I'd rather have ten years of superhypermost than live to be seventy sitting in some goddam chair watching TV." Everywhere, kids sprouted long hair; donned beads, peace medallions, and bell-bottoms; and turned almost every garage into a rehearsal studio for a rock band or a folk group. Where there were kids, there was, as always, music. Throughout this decade, as never before, youth seemed to act out its age-old drama of rebellion to the accompaniment of its own self-performed signature theme music. A protest rally at the Washington Monument, for example, might turn into a cluster of groups, each gathered around a guitar-playing activist, bundled up in an old army surplus jacket, plunking an instrument plastered with peace symbols and slogans. The songs would be the old standby courage-builders of the movement, thrown once again into the night – "We Shall Overcome" or "Blowin' in the Wind" or "Gonna Let My Little Light Shine."

Sixties music wasn't all grim and heavy. When they weren't at the barricades, the sixties musicians turned out some unforgettable ballads: Simon & Garfunkel did "Mrs. Robinson" and "Bridge Over Troubled Water," and Arlo Guthrie sang his haunting version of "City of New Orleans" – and his hilarious "Alice's Restaurant." The rock musical *Hair* electrified theatergoers, and from it songs such as "Hair" and "Let the Sun Shine In" made the pop scene.

But to a powerful extent, the thrum of the guitar and the jingle of the tambourine had become fife and drum to a restless generation, summoning the kids. And they came, to places like the Pentagon, and to Selma, and to happier spots, too. In Woodstock, New York, in 1969 the flower children partied for a long, rainy – and drug-soaked – weekend of ecstatic wonderment, listening to their heroes. But the act the world remembers is the show the mob of nearly half a million put on by itself there in those muddy acres of pastureland: three days of peace and love, no violence, just good vibes, man.

The music summoned them to sadder, uglier gatherings, too. In Altamont, California, as at Woodstock, thousands gathered for a concert. But at Altamont, pool cue–swinging Hell's Angels "security" forces went amok. And on the streets of Chicago, in 1968, police rioted also, battering the kids who had come to the Democratic convention, that cataclysmic confrontation with the Establishment for which all the music had been just an overture.

Flower power lost that battle, but as Sonny and Cher put it in their ballad of the time, "The Beat Goes On," and in the end, the kids won their war. And their joyous, mournful beat still does go on, echoing now nearly three decades later into a world it helped to change.

*Ordinarily staid, proper Londoners got out of line just like everybody else and tried to crash the gate for a glimpse when the Beatles visited Buckingham Palace to pick up their medals from the queen making them members of the Order of the British Empire. Said Paul of the palace, "a keen pad," and of the queen, "she was just like a mum to us."*
1965, Central Press, London

*The Beatles began a fifteen-day visit to the United States in February 1964 and were followed from city to city by teenage pandemonium. They made their smash American debut on Ed Sullivan's TV show, setting a record for the highest viewer ratings up to that time.*
< 1964, CBS

During their 1964 visit to New York City, the Beatles stayed
at the Plaza Hotel, which was usually surrounded by their
shrieking fans. After a performance one fan explained,
"We don't come to hear them, really. We have their records.
We come to scream at them." The Beatles loved it.
1964, Arthur Schatz

In Miami, the Beatles—from left, Paul
McCartney, George Harrison, John Lennon,
and Ringo Starr—jumped into an unheated
pool and burst into song for the photographer. They sold more records and made more
money than had any other performers
before them.
1964, John Loengard

John Lennon strikes a Sgt. Pepperish pose in
his frogged bandmaster's jacket.
1967, Henry Grossman >

A rare moment of quiet is shared by the Who, a British rock group known for its exuberance on stage. The destruction of musical instruments was the traditional ending to a performance, an expensive but effective way of avoiding encores. They are, from left: Keith Moon, Roger Daltrey, Peter Townshend, and John Entwistle.
<< 1968, Art Kane

At a beach near Miami, and repeated on almost every beach in America and in much of Europe, crowds of teenagers swarm to swim, sunbathe, and be turned on by a new kind of music—a mix of American rock and roll and the Beatles sound. It reverberated in the thousands of discotheques that erupted across the country.
1965, Lynn Pelham

Harry Belafonte, Leon Bibb, and Joan Baez sing on the steps of the State Capitol in Montgomery, Alabama. The celebration marked the successful conclusion of a five-day march from Selma, Alabama, to Montgomery to encourage voter registration.
1965, Charles Moore from Black Star

Bob Dylan performs at a Madison Square Garden rock concert. He was one of the most important figures in the music of the sixties. His songs became the sound of protest and the spirit of civil rights and opposition to the war. Dylan's "Blowin' in the Wind" and "The Times They Are A-Changin'" were anthems for the youth movement, the finest expression of its mood and feeling.
1971, Bill Ray

The age of Aquarius came to Broadway on April 29, 1968, with the opening of Hair, the first pop-rock musical. The young and spirited cast joined in a primordial celebration of unfettered existence, embracing drugs, protesting war, and preaching love and sexual freedom. The show was noted for its nude scene and its catchy contemporary score.
1968, Ralph Morse >>

Sheer essence of sixties disco: the music was a deafening force field of sound, pulsating with a sensual beat that made dancing irresistible, with the lights strobing through a thin haze of smoke. The place had a name like Le Bison, if it was Chicago, or Studio 54 in New York.
< 1969, Vernon Merritt III

Dancers in a suspended cage demonstrate the moves in this West Hollywood discotheque called Whiskey a Go Go, where customers waited three hours to squeeze in and do the hot new wriggle, the watusi.
< 1964, Julian Wasser

An uninhibited and unencumbered young couple enjoy the sunshine and freedom of a rock festival in Amador, California. 1970, Robert Garro

It was advertised as the Woodstock Music and Art Fair,
"three days of peace and music." The remarkable thing is that
is exactly what it was. The event drew close to a half million
young people to a thirty-five-acre area in the Catskill village
of Bethel, New York, with woefully inadequate food, shelter,
and sanitation. A two-day rainstorm turned the field into a
sea of mud. The air was redolent of marijuana smoke, and
drugs were everywhere. There was little or no crime. A feeling of camaraderie and love and the joy of living for the
moment in a world that seemed all theirs dominated the
event. There was peace and there was music – Janis Joplin,
Jimi Hendrix, Joan Baez, Grace Slick, Arlo Guthrie, and
many others – almost continuously day and night.
1969, John Dominis

A sodden group seeks protection from pelting rain at
Woodstock under a sheet of plywood supported on the heads
of the tallest.
< 1969, John Dominis

*English rock guitarist Noel Redding makes music. Redding performed with the Jimi Hendrix Experience, which LIFE called "rock's miscegenation of black and white, of Beatles and soul, of taunting challenge and response."*
1968, Linda Eastman

*A drummer at Woodstock hammers out the beat.*
1969, Bill Eppridge

*After her performance at the Woodstock festival, Janis Joplin closes her eyes in exhaustion. She was considered the top white female blues singer of the sixties and, by some, one of the greatest of all time. Often raucous and out of control, Joplin nevertheless delivered the kind of spirited performance that made her unforgettable. She died in 1970 at the age of twenty-seven from an overdose of heroin.*
1969, Tucker Ranson >

# LIFE: The '60s

## *Protest*

As if hurtling free from the quietude of the fifties, dissidents during the sixties let fly a staccato drumroll of protests that kept the nation writhing in turmoil throughout much of the decade. LIFE, in a special issue published in 1969, looked back at the preceding era, marveled wryly that the period had been "perhaps richer in experience than any other that Americans have lived through," and labeled it "the decade of tumult and change."

The early sixties, LIFE's editors said, had been marked by a "brisk feeling of hope, a generally optimistic and energetic shift from the calm of the late '50's." But then, they reported, "in a growing swell of demands for extreme and immediate change, the second part of the decade exploded—over race, youth, violence, life-styles, and, above all, the Vietnam war."

Techniques of protest devised and perfected by the activists in the civil rights movement—methods of passive resistance that were copied from Gandhi—were adapted by opponents of the war in Vietnam. The civil rights demonstrations that had begun in 1955 as a lone black woman refused to give up her seat to a white on an Alabama bus grew to groups of students refusing to leave lunch counters where they were denied service, and then to whole busloads of sympathizers, "Freedom Riders," assaulting the barriers of America's apartheid. Perhaps the grandest of the era's protests was the March on Washington in 1963, where Dr. Martin Luther King, Jr., told a crowd of more than two hundred thousand—the largest civil rights demonstration in history—of his dream "that one day this nation will rise up and live out the true meaning of its creed." But there were many other demonstrations, too. Big ones such as the Poor People's Campaign in 1968, where antipoverty demonstrators, mostly blacks, established a shantytown called Resurrection City on the mall in Washington. And little ones, such as James Meredith's walk, alone, across Mississippi in 1966 to encourage black voter registration as well as to demonstrate that he had no fear to return to the place where, in 1962, he had led a battle to integrate the university. Then, getting Meredith into Ole Miss had required three hundred U.S. marshals, five thousand soldiers and National Guardsmen, and cost two lives before the fifteen-hour riot had ended. This time, Meredith didn't succeed: he was wounded from ambush by a shotgun blast. But the demonstrations continued.

Antiwar demonstrators, too, increased in numbers as the casualties in Vietnam mounted—only one hundred or so demonstrators turned out for an antiwar rally in Boston in 1965; but by 1969, opposition had spread and deepened to the extent that an antiwar demonstration there drew one hundred thousand. Marchers chanting "Hell, no, we won't go"—some dressed as skeletons, some carrying coffins, masked grotesquely as caricatures of Johnson and Nixon—bearing placards, all became common sights on the streets and the federal plazas of the nation's cities. Sometimes protesters gathered to burn their draft cards. Across the country, campuses such as Harvard, Columbia, and Berkeley were wracked, often closed down, as student demonstrators took possession of office buildings to make their stand.

Countless acts of individual protest occurred as well, from Joan Baez's refusal to pay that part of her income tax that she calculated went to support the war, to the public suicide of Norman Morrison, a Quaker activist who put his child down at the edge of a parking lot at the Pentagon and then set himself afire.

The right to peaceable assembly for the redress of grievances, of course, is a key provision of the U.S. Constitution, inscribed in the Bill of Rights. But exercising that right, privately and publicly, often required great courage. There were many in the country to whom the notion of protest was anathema, somehow un-American, the product of "outside agitators." Often, the most vehement opposition to the demonstrators came from the police—and to many of the protesters, the cops were "the pigs." In the South, demonstrators were treated viciously, not only by the Ku Klux Klan and other hate groups, but in many cases by local law enforcement officials as well. Likewise, in many areas opponents of the war in Vietnam were regarded as traitors, their public demonstrations undermining the morale of our troops in the field—and thus aiding and abetting the enemy.

The vehemence of the antiwar demonstrations continued, however, abating at last when U.S. troop withdrawals began in Vietnam. Home-front gunfire and police billies, too, did much to quell the demonstrators: as the new decade got under way, police in 1970 killed two students protesting the war at Jackson State University in Mississippi; National Guardsmen at Kent State opened fire on demonstrators in what LIFE called an act of "senseless and brutal point blank murder," killing four and wounding nine. Many in the U.S. cheered; one reader wrote LIFE to say the Kent State shootings were a "valuable object lesson" to the students.

In the end, the protesters must be credited with bringing about vast changes in American life and thought. By focusing national attention on what had been the shameful regional practice of segregation, they forced the federal government to enforce existing laws and pressured the Congress to enact new ones, protecting the rights of blacks. By spotlighting the terrible costs in human life, and the futility, of the war in Vietnam, both of which the government had attempted to conceal, the activists marshaled opposition that eventually brought American involvement to an end. The war protesters caused Lyndon Johnson to decide not to run for President in 1968 and made it expedient for Richard Nixon to campaign on a promise to wind down the war.

By taking to the streets, the antiwar and the civil rights activists showed partisans of many other causes, such as women's rights, homosexual rights, environmental preservation, legalizing or abolishing abortion, and countless others, that protest can be heard in America—just as the Founding Fathers had intended.

Demonstrations convulsed campuses across the nation throughout the decade. Here, resting amid paintings and sculpture in
an administration building they seized, student protesters
demonstrate at Harvard against ROTC and university
expansion into adjacent slums at the cost of low-income
housing, and in support of black studies.
< 1969, Timothy Carlson

Student demonstrators at Harvard convene in the faculty
room of the university's administration building and debate
how to handle the police if they come. Later that night they
decided on nonviolence. But Harvard president Nathan M.
Pusey called for help, and the next day, in riot helmets
and carrying billies, the Cambridge police, who usually
ignore undergraduate ruckuses in Harvard Yard, ousted
the squatters.
< 1969, Timothy Carlson

Gas masks and fixed bayonets were equipment of the day at
Berkeley when students protested by Sather Gate against the
ouster of seventy-five hippies from a People's Park in a vacant
lot owned by the University of California. Before it ended, the
National Guard, police, and sheriff's deputies used shotguns
and tear gas – sprayed from a helicopter. Many students were
injured and one bystander was killed.
1969, Tom Tracy

Stunned and disbelieving, a young woman kneels beside the body of a Kent State student, killed by a National Guardsman's bullet. Ohio governor James A. Rhodes had ordered the Guard on campus after students demonstrating against the war smashed windows in town and set fire to ROTC headquarters. Students and troops formed skirmish lines that shifted back and forth. The students, not knowing that Ohio, unlike most states, permitted its Guard to use live ammunition, kept pelting the troops with sticks and stones even when the soldiers aimed their rifles. A thirteen-second fusillade left four students dead and nine wounded.

1970, John Paul Filo for *The Tarentum Valley News Dispatch*

The Black Panther Party for Self-Defense, of Oakland, California, believed, as their minister of defense, Huey P. Newton, put it, that power came from the barrel of a gun. Or, as Chairman Bobby Seale expressed it, "All we want is a cool, clear, fresh drink of water. But we can't get a cool, clear, fresh drink of water 'cause there's a hog in the stream, so we're gonna have to get the hog out of the stream or die trying." The hog in the rhetoric was white America. Nonetheless, a lot of Yale students turned out for a rally supporting the gun-toting Panthers and Seale, who packed a .45.

1970, Lee Balterman >

A battle-jacketed speaker harangues the crowd at the Panther
rally at Yale. His "Free Huey" button shows his sympathy
for Black Panther Huey P. Newton, convicted in California for
murder in the shooting of an Oakland policeman. Newton
was freed by an appeals court.
< 1970, Lee Balterman

Thousands marched in Washington, D.C., to demonstrate
their opposition to the war in Vietnam. Here, one marcher
lights his draft card.
1967, Richard Swanson

On the fiftieth anniversary of the passage of the Nineteenth
Amendment, which granted women the right to vote, a large
parade of enthusiastic and resolute women sets off down Fifth
Avenue in New York City. The precision of their marching
style may have left something to be desired, but there was no
questioning the rhythm, grace, and strength of their line as it
moved down the avenue.
1970, John Olson >>

Hair, headbands, natural fibers, leather—and plenty of sincere skin—were key elements of the sixties style, in evidence wherever youth gathered.
1969, Vernon Merritt III

Old Glory served one hairy hippie as a robe at a so-called Be-in in New York City's Central Park. The scene was so laid-back, however, that it was perfectly okay to come dressed as a square, too, clad in natural-shoulder, button-down Ivy League style.
1969, Steve Schapiro

*Male or female, a ring in the lobe was groovy, and the folk art Ojo de Dios – "Eye of God" – yarn sculpture, universal talisman of good vibes, was a cutting-edge accoutrement to bring along to a Central Park Be-in. Both revealed where you were coming from – and it wasn't Establishment.*
1969, Steve Schapiro

121

# LIFE: The '60s

## *Fads and Fashions*

America had seen fads before, but this time just about *everything* seemed to go utterly crazy all at once — clothes, behavior, manners, morals. Suddenly, it seemed, there was just a whole new way of life, which was only appropriate, after all — wasn't this a brand-new era in America?

Underlying these massive changes in the topography of American life were some powerful seismic social forces — and some mighty potent chemicals, as well: mind-bending drugs, which by the end of the decade had appeared everywhere, from grammar school playgrounds to corporate corridors. There were uppers — amphetamines, speed; and there were downers — barbiturates. There were tranquilizers — devilishly easier to begin taking than to quit. And then there was the really weird stuff, such as mescaline and peyote. And old standbys, such as heroin, cocaine, and of course, marijuana. Reefer, an earlier generation had called it. Sixties kids called it grass. It added a dash of adventure to brownies.

But a whole new thing was out there now, too, a drug so potent, so unbelievably powerful, that just one drop of it, just a dab on a sugar cube, a touch of it on a piece of blotting paper, and this new man-made drug called LSD — for *ly*sergic acid *d*iethylamide — would take you farther out, and deeper in, on bizarre hallucinogenic journeys called trips, than anybody had ever gone before. Some LSD trippers just didn't come back at all, having killed themselves while under the thrall of this powerful drug that made them think they could fly off balconies or walk through locomotives.

Another kind of pharmaceutical was changing things, too — the pill, which prevented the women who took it from becoming pregnant. The pill revolutionized the role of women in society, launching a new chapter in the feminine drive toward full equality with men. The new freedom from the repercussions of biology opened the way for a new era in sexual behavior, and with new mores came a new morality for many. As the sixties had dawned, a major campus issue at sophisticated Ivy League schools like Columbia had been how far the door could be left open during a young woman's visit to a room in the men's dorm. But 1969 just closed the door altogether and grappled, as men and women living together in the dorms became accepted.

A breeze of earnestness blew through the land, fueled by the meditative introspection that accompanied the drug scene. The disheveled beatniks of the fifties, with their jaded nihilism, gave way to terribly sincere hippies in gaudily tie-dyed bell-bottoms and T-shirts who spoke winsomely of finding their own space. Across the country, from Haight-Ashbury to Greenwich Village, decked out in miniskirts and nehru jackets, aglitter with peace medallions and clattering beads, hippies, many of them hitchhiking, spread the message and the culture of flower power. Men sprouted pigtails and vans blossomed with multi colored floral paint jobs.

But not everybody joined this unconventional group — some upward strivers wore the new double-knit fabrics and on their feet sported a glossy new artificial leather, Corfam. The counter culture types, however — the granola-munching, granny glasses–wearing, back-to-the-landers — sneered at such test-tube products as they snuggled deeper into their natural-fiber ponchos, wriggled their toes in their heelless earth sandals, and holed up in their yurts. The whole country seemed divided up into camps, all of them with members looking as if they were headed for a costume ball, as people donned the garb they thought best expressed where they stood, how they felt, what they believed in, who they were—and who they wanted to be. The movie *The Graduate* dramatized the plight of the young American torn between "plastics" and that other world, where youth lived in communes and read *The Greening of America.*

This notion that there was an inner, secret self that you had to seek out to discover was something new in this astonishing decade. Hardly surprising, then, that with this notion came an epidemic of powerful ideologies, from the driving idealism of the New Frontier to bizarre Eastern cults. Young and old Americans alike signed up to go abroad and help foster the spread of democracy by digging sewer lines and teaching English in the Peace Corps. They joined VISTA to go into the urban and rural slums as teachers. Some took off for ashrams, communities like those started by the Hinduist Hare Krishnas, which sprouted in the rural countrysides, and learned to chant their mantras. "Om," was the word, or something like it, as the tambourines jingled and the sitars whined.

And at the same time, in the swampy bottomlands of the American soul, the American Nazi party and the National Association for the Advancement of White People blossomed, too, along with older hate groups such as the Ku Klux Klan. But in the horror-sated sixties, evil, even a multiple killer, had to have some kind of spectacularly kinky style, had to be a Charles Manson or a Richard Speck, to capture much lasting public attention. As pop artist Andy Warhol declared wryly, *everybody* would be famous—but for only fifteen minutes. With Warhol's mocking celebrations of the banal—giant replications of Campbell's soup labels, for example—and the serpentine weirdnesses of Peter Max, popular art became pop art and then op art. It was seeking meaning in nothingness, value in everything.

The put-on was everywhere, as the mordant tone of irony pervaded American life.

And youth, these heady new days, was seen and heard and paid attention to, suddenly recognized as a major new market for goods, as demanding consumers, as a prospective and fearsome new political force. To be young in the sixties no longer meant to be callow, inexperienced. It meant being vigorous, hopeful, energetic, strong, free—and skeptical: Never Trust Anybody Over Thirty was the motto of a generation.

As always in such times of cataclysmic change, Americans sought more keenly than ever to achieve some individual identity. That's who all those folks were, wearing those crazy getups: free spirits, all, seekers after the American dream of life, liberty, and the pursuit of happiness—sixties style.

A young woman forlornly tries to comfort her husband and his brother. All three are heroin addicts. By now there is no way left but crime for them to get the money to support their habit. Their hopelessness and the specter of the end adds momentum to the downward spiral of their lives.
1965, Bill Eppridge

In a Manhattan detective squad room, a fifteen-year-old picked up by police as a runaway talks with her father in Washington, D.C. He came to get her that night. But tens of thousands more like her were on the nation's streets, LIFE reported.
1967, I. C. Rapoport

*Allen Ginsberg, forty, poet laureate of the Beat generation,*
*author of "Howl," takes tea.*
1966, John Loengard

*Ten-minute "eyeballing" sessions increase the "love-level"
of encounter group clients in Palm Springs, California, just a
few of thousands of Americans in the Human Potential
Movement seeking to unlock the power of their inner selves.
"Warmth and love," this group believed, "need not mean
sex" – and clothes, they felt, were "the modern mask, often a
way to keep ourselves and others at a distance emotionally."*
1968, Ralph Crane

*Harvard University fired psychologist Timothy Leary for his
experiments with lysergic acid diethylamide, LSD, a powerful
hallucinogen. But to the drug's enthusiastic fans, he was
a guru.*
< 1962, Lawrence Schiller

Peter Max, a prolific artist and entrepreneur, is surrounded by
his psychedelic posters and designs that capture the feeling of
the pop generation in the age of Aquarius.
1967, Yale Joel

Communal living flourished in the U.S. in the late sixties
when young pioneers, a majority of them dropouts from big
cities, sought to escape what they regarded as meaningless
occupations, superficial values, and rootlessness. These members of a commune have been living on this southern Oregon
site for over a year.
< 1969, John Olson

Long hair, miniskirts, youth, and a clean-cut
casualness were some of the elements in what
came to be known as the New York look.
1969, Vernon Merritt III

Black Is Beautiful began as a militant slogan, but by 1968
it had become a fashion statement. Pride in black culture
inspired African designs like this jewelry and Afro wig, mod-
eled by Roanne Nesbitt.
< 1968, Yale Joel

*This could be any summer day on any of the beaches in the
Los Angeles area.*
1970, Co Rentmeester

*At the 1960 Olympics in Rome, Wilma
Rudolph, twenty, won the women's one-
hundred-meter dash with a final burst of
speed, setting a record of eleven seconds.
Rudolph, winner of three gold medals at the
Games, had been so badly crippled by a
series of childhood illnesses that she had not
been able to walk unaided until she was
eleven years old.*
1960, Mark Kauffman

*Floating downstream in an inner tube on Wisconsin's Apple River is a quiet and enduring pleasure.*
1970, © Gerald Brimacombe

*Manuel Capetillo, a bullfighter from Guadalajara, Mexico, dresses for the bullring while his three-year-old son and inseparable companion, Memo, tries on his hat.*
1961, Peter Anderson from Black Star

*With skill and grace, Kathy Flicker, fourteen, executes a dive that achieves a rare ten-point score, at Princeton's Dillon Gym pool. She created a symmetrical V in the water, one of the signs of a perfect entry.*
1962, George Silk

*Designed by Ted Hood, the radical twelve-meter yacht* Nefertiti *exhibited grace, beauty, and power. It did not win the competition to become the eighteenth defender of the America's Cup but is still remembered for its impressive performance and red-topped spinnaker.*
1962, George Silk >

San Francisco Giants' superstar Willie Mays
doffs his cap to applauding fans after helping
the team beat Houston with his 501st
home run.
1965, Bob Gomel

Los Angeles Dodgers' pitcher Sandy Koufax
prepares to launch his fastball.
1963, Leigh Wiener

New York Yankee sluggers Mickey Mantle
(left) and Roger Maris battled to break the
record of sixty home runs in one season set in
1927 by another Yankee, Babe Ruth. (The
background photo of the Babe is by William
C. Greene of the New York World-Telegram.)
Maris finally hit his sixty-first on the last
day of the 1961 season — which had been
increased by eight more games than in
Ruth's day.
< 1961, © Philippe Halsman

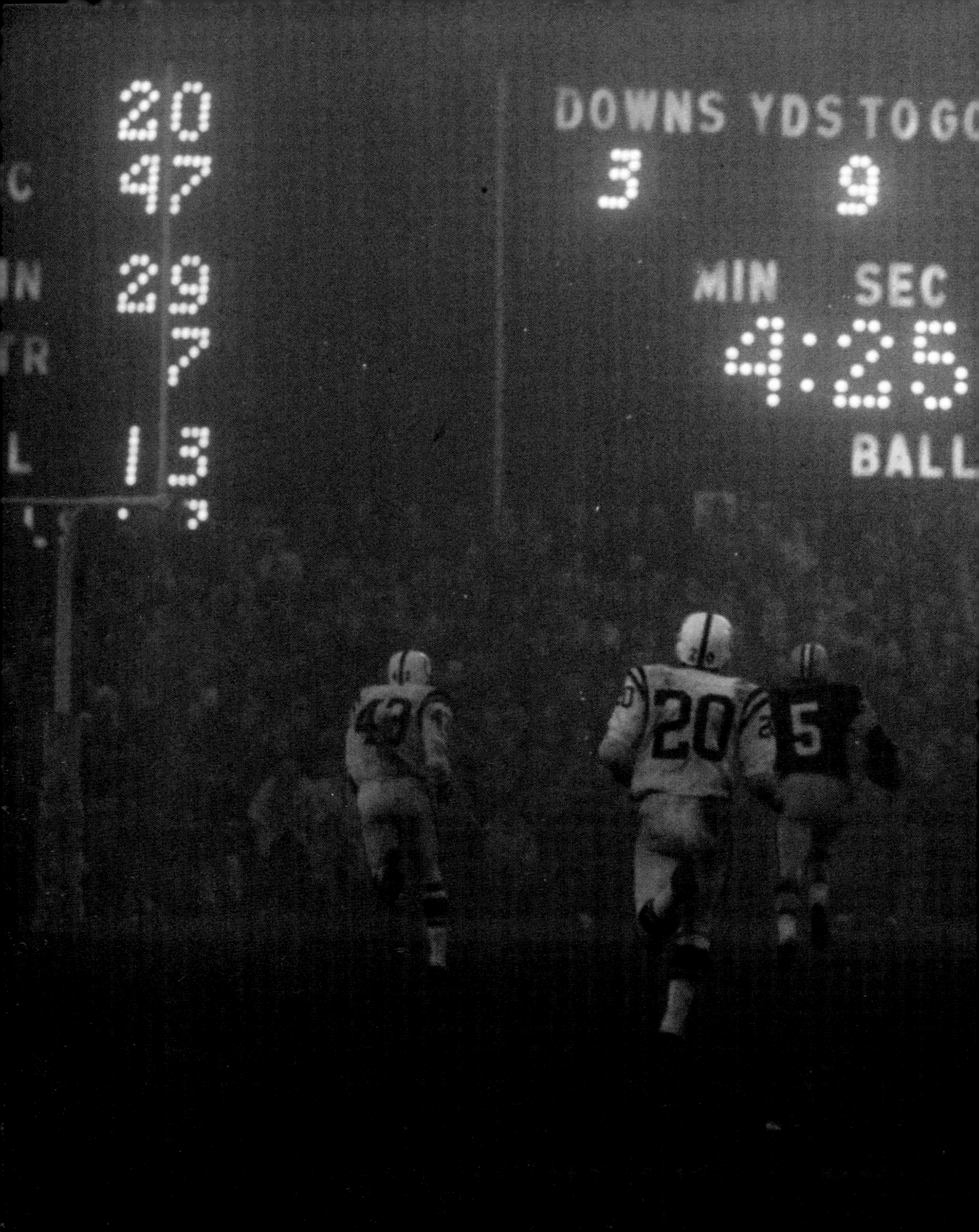
20
47
29
7
13
DOWNS YDS
3
9
MIN SEC
4:25
BALL
20
5

Showing the effects of a soggy day in Cleveland's Municipal
Stadium, the Browns' front four—from left, Walter Johnson,
Dick Modzelewski, Paul Wiggin, and Jim Houston—await the
Green Bay Packers' next play.
1965, Arthur Rickerby

In Pittsburgh, dazed and bleeding after being
hit by a bruising tackle, New York Giants'
quarterback Y. A. Tittle, thirty-eight, realizes
that his playing days are probably coming to
an end. Survivor of seventeen years of pro
football, Tittle played out the season, but it
was his last.
1964, Morris Berman

At Baltimore's Memorial Stadium, Green
Bay Packers' Paul Hornung (number 5)
eludes the Colts' defense to score his fifth
touchdown of the game, driving the Packers
to a 42–27 victory.
<< 1965, Arthur Rickerby

In the locker room after the game, "Broadway
Joe" Namath toasts the New York Jets' Super
Bowl victory, which he quarterbacked over
the Baltimore Colts.
1969, Ken Regan—Camera 5 >

*In Miami Beach, Muhammad Ali (formerly Cassius Clay)
exults as his opponent, Sonny Liston, is unable to come out
for the seventh round, thereby ceding to Ali the heavyweight
championship of the world. At twenty-two, Ali became the
second-youngest holder of the title in the history of the sport.*
1964, Herb Scharfman

*Heavyweight champ Sonny Liston (right) focuses his fearsome scowl on Floyd Patterson at the weigh-in for their title fight in Las Vegas. That night in the ring, Patterson folded in just a little over two minutes.*
1963, Bill Ray

*Novelist and sometime boxing writer Norman Mailer shows he's no sissy, arm wrestling Muhammad Ali to a draw in San Juan, Puerto Rico. Mailer's training: two Zombie cocktails before the match.*
1965, Marvin W. Schwartz, *The San Juan Star*

144

*Tennis great Arthur Ashe gets airborne to return a backhand shot with power and agility.*
< 1965, Bob Gomel

*Louis Armstrong, born and raised in New Orleans, played a few seasons in clubs and on Mississippi riverboats before leaving for Chicago and New York, where his creative gifts and technical skills overwhelmed the jazz musicians of his day. The best-known trumpeter of his generation, Satchmo's raspy voice was also unforgettable, evidenced in his now classic version of "Hello, Dolly!"*
1966, © Philippe Halsman

Holding the script of his last movie, The
Misfits, *Clark Gable, fifty-nine, reminisces in
his dressing room. Only weeks later, he died
of a heart attack.*
1960, Eve Arnold for Magnum

*With a characteristic touch of class – dressed in a Jean Louis
sheath and wearing jewels worth $170,000 – Gloria Swanson
says good-bye to the Roxy Theater in Manhattan, reduced to
rubble by the wrecker's ball. She had been guest of honor at
the gala opening of the $11 million movie palace in 1927.*
1960, Eliot Elisofon >

Geraldine Page's fading movie star and Paul Newman's self-seeking gigolo are compelling though unsavory characters in Tennessee Williams's play Sweet Bird of Youth. Page gave what is generally considered to be the finest performance of her career, and Newman, in one of his few stage roles, was memorable.
1959, Gordon Parks

Hollywood legend Marilyn Monroe poses for a photograph in July 1962, a month before her death.
1962, Allan Grant

Elizabeth Taylor chats with her soon-to-be fifth husband, Richard Burton, during a time-out in the filming of Cleopatra. Taylor, in the title role, and Burton, as Mark Antony, gave as intense performances offscreen as on.
1962, Paul Schutzer >

*Fellow actor Roddy McDowall took this photograph of Sir Laurence Olivier as he prepares for his performance in Shakespeare's* Othello *in London. Olivier, first director of Britain's Royal National Theatre, is commonly regarded as the greatest actor of our time.*
1964, Roddy McDowall

*Life never ran smoothly for Lucille Ball in her TV series "I Love Lucy." Every episode ended with Lucy caught up in a complicated, outrageously involved, hilarious mess. In the scene shown here – a takeoff on an early silent movie serial,* The Perils of Pauline – *Lucy plummets into the Grand Canyon. The beloved comedienne died in April 1989 at the age of seventy-seven.*
1962, Leonard McCombe

*Director Alfred Hitchcock pretends to prepare to dine on one*
*of his feathered stars while two others attack Tippi Hedren,*
*just as they did in the spine-tingling film* The Birds.
1963, © Philippe Halsman

Bob Hope wears an Indian headdress presented by women
of Oklahoma State University. The veteran entertainer – he
made his Broadway debut in 1927 – also has been honored
three times by Congress and decorated by Presidents Eisenhower, Kennedy, and Johnson.
1962, Allan Grant

Richard Kiley (left) as Don Quixote and Irving Jacobson
as Sancho Panza ride in search of windmills in Man of
La Mancha.
1966, Henry Groskinsky >

Singer Pearl Bailey reigned as Dolly in an all-black cast production of the popular musical Hello, Dolly!
< 1967, John Dominis

At work in his Manhattan loft, abstract artist Ad Reinhardt touches a brush to one of his starkly minimalist canvases. His art, he said, is "non-objective, non-figurative, non-imagist, non-expressionist, non-subjective. Fine art can only be defined as exclusive, negative, absolute and timeless."
1966, John Loengard

Samuel Beckett avoided publicity and declined all interviews. When Beckett won the Nobel Prize for Literature in 1969, he consented to appear for photographs – of which this is one – but sat in silence during the picture-taking. When an apology was made for disturbing him, the Irish playwright responded, "That's all right. I understand" – and then returned to his silence.

1969, Hubert Le Campion

Edward Villella dances the title role in The Prodigal Son, a ballet based on the biblical story, choreographed by George Balanchine, director of the New York City Ballet. A very athletic dancer, Villella performed in a bravura style, brilliant and daring, and punctuated with soaring leaps of dramatic force and speed.

< 1969, Bill Eppridge

Children watching the Guignol puppet show
in the Parc de Montsouris in Paris react
with Gallic expressiveness at the high point
of the drama – the slaying of the dragon.
1963, Alfred Eisenstaedt

Seven-year-old Christopher Wilson studies
the result of blowing air through a pipe into
a jar of water. His small boy's curiosity about
the natural world had free rein because his
backyard was woods and his front yard a
Puget Sound beach that at high tide was
under six feet of water.
1961, Steven C. Wilson/Entheos

*A graceful child, wearing a crown of blossoms, carries a*
*bouquet to a fiesta in Guanajuato, Mexico.*
1968, John Dominis

*In Los Angeles, seventy-eight-year-old Shichizo Takeda, a Japanese movie extra, enjoys working out on a trampoline.*
1960, Ralph Crane

*A freighter of the Peninsular and Oriental Steam Navigation Company – the P&O for short – lies at anchor in Hong Kong after unloading cargo. Local workmen make interesting calligraphy on the ship's hull as they scrape and undercoat rust spots.*
< 1962, John Dominis

*Workmen excavate 150-foot-deep canyons in which to lay
conduits for diverting water from the Niagara River. The
rerouting was part of a multimillion-dollar power project in
upstate New York.*
1960, Fritz Goro

*The Haughwout Building on lower Broadway in New York
City is considered one of the best surviving examples of cast-
iron construction, popular in the second half of the 1800s.
Prefabricated sections were shipped to the building site and
bolted together in a few weeks. Such structures were strong,
inexpensive, and fire resistant.*
< 1965, Evelyn Hofer

*This 108-foot-high framework for a cathedral
burst like a concrete flower through the red
earth of Brasília, the made-to-order capital
of Brazil. Oscar Niemeyer was the architect
of this and the other major buildings of the
city, built in 1960.*
1961, Dmitri Kessel >>

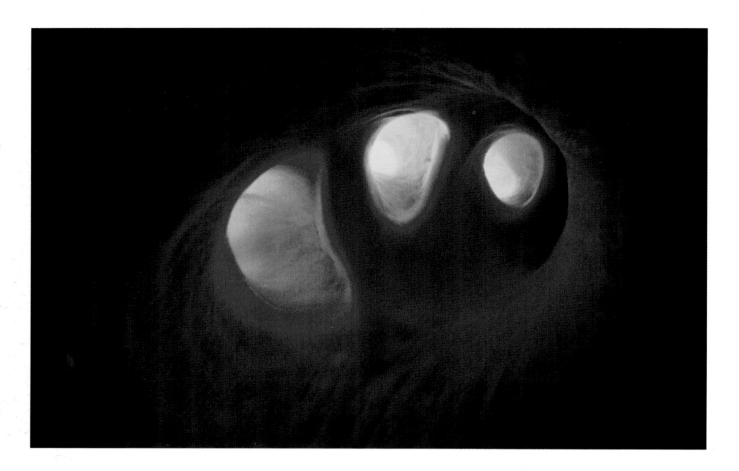

The three photographs on these pages are by Swedish photographer Lennart Nilsson, who specialized in producing never-before-seen views of the interior of the human body. This photograph of the aortic arch of a one-year-old has been magnified forty times. The three vessels whose openings are shown here carried blood to the arms and head.
1968, Lennart Nilsson

The bone plates of the mature human skull (shown backlit) are rigid, but before birth they are loosely joined so that the skull may compress during delivery and then expand as the brain increases in size.
1969, Lennart Nilsson

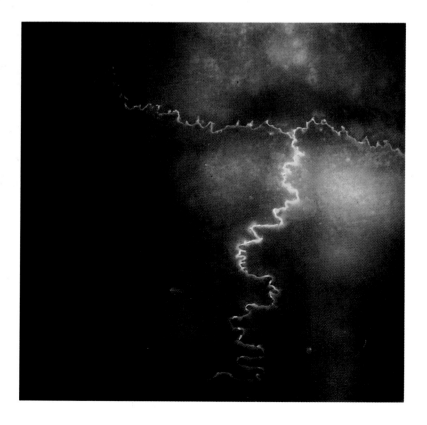

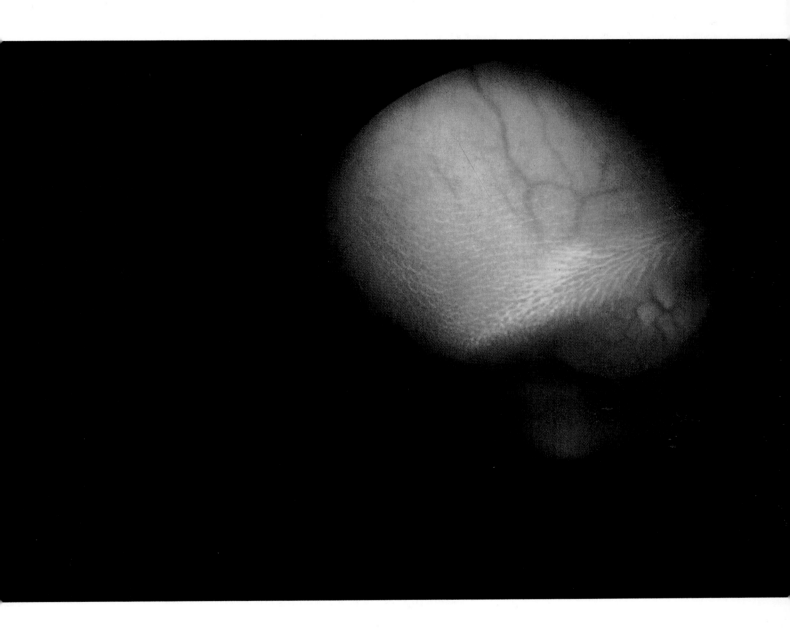

*This is the first photograph ever made of a living embryo inside its mother's womb. Its landmark importance has been compared to that of the first photographs taken of the far side of the moon, in 1959. Using specially designed instruments, Nilsson was able to photograph this fifteen-week-old embryo from a distance of one inch. In approximately twenty-five more weeks, a baby will be born, having developed from a fertilized egg into a being of some two hundred million cells.*
1965, Lennart Nilsson

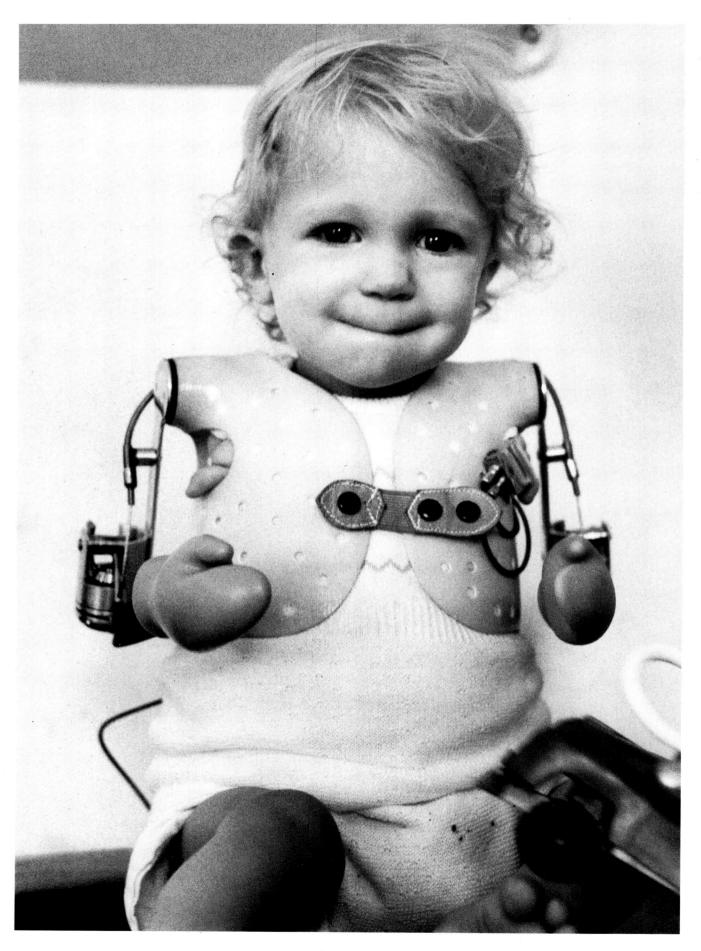

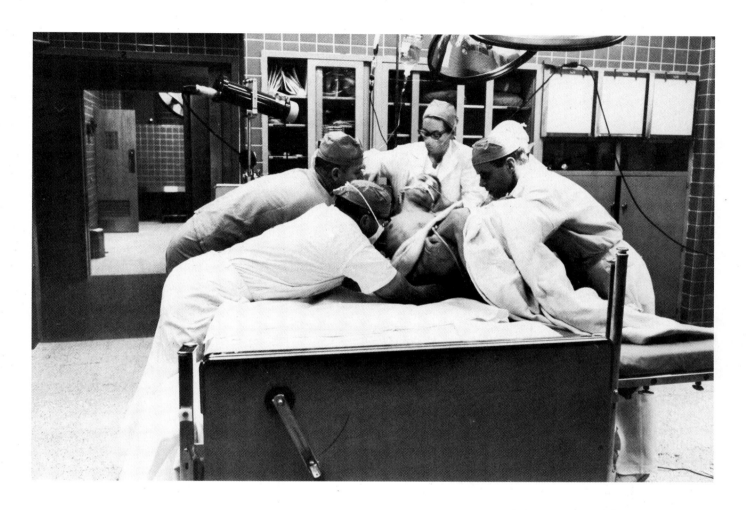

After a 140-minute kidney transplant operation, a team of
doctors and aides at Ohio's Cleveland Clinic gently lift Wolf
Sturmer, a thirty-four-year-old Indiana teacher, onto a bed in
the operating room to be wheeled into the intensive care unit.
This was one of the earliest kidney transplant operations.
1965, Ralph Morse

This German baby girl, not yet two, is "unaware she is not
like the rest of life she sees," LIFE reported, in a story detail-
ing the casualties of the tranquilizer-sleeping pill thalido-
mide. The drug caused some pregnant mothers to give birth
to children afflicted with phocomelia—deformed limbs.
< 1962, Stan Wayman

This glittering handful of gemlike electronic parts could
equal the performance of a whole closetful of conventional
vacuum tubes, LIFE explained in a story heralding the age of
solid-state microchips. Most of these parts were destined for
the innards of another new wonder: computers.
1960, Fritz Goro

There has always been a special beauty in well-designed
machinery, as is illustrated by this much-enlarged photograph of a switching unit in a 1967 computer.
1967, Henry Groskinsky >

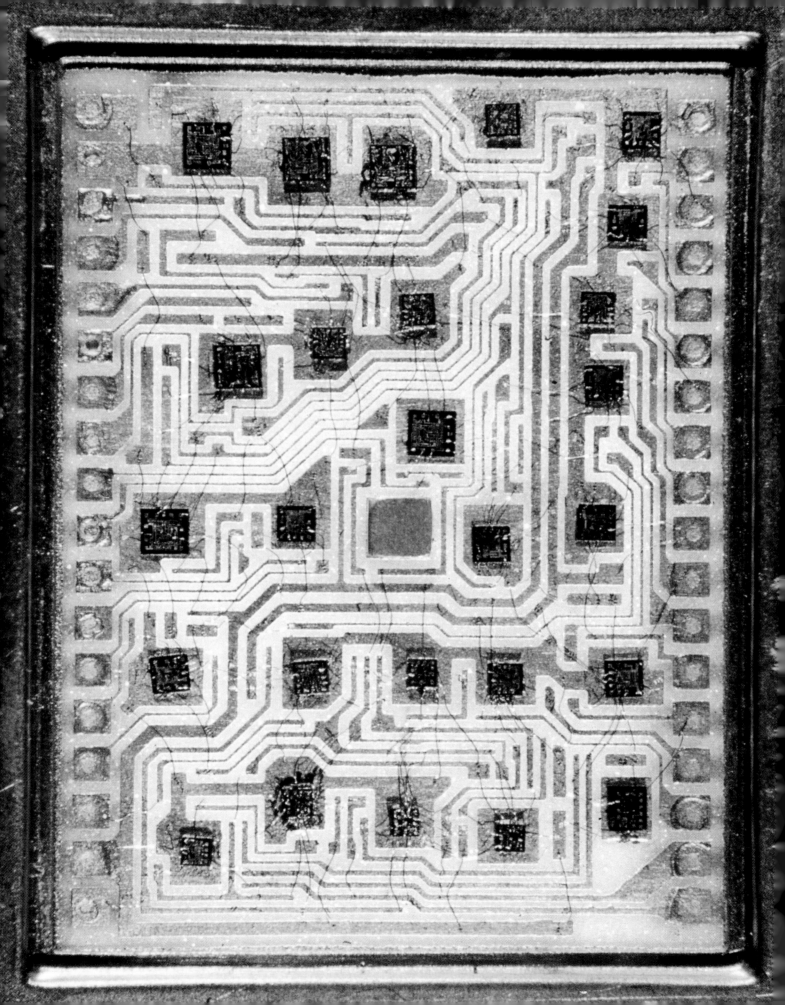

# LIFE: The '60s

## *Space*

Throughout the sixties, while the very linchpins of the nation seemed to be stressed to the breaking point with riots and assassinations and dissent, one group of Americans functioned with cool, precise courage and mostly spectacular success. At Cape Canaveral—after 1963 called Cape Kennedy in honor of the President who put the impetus of his office behind the work done there—the rockets blasted off, carrying American astronauts into space again and again until the marvelous, incredible feats became almost, but never quite, routine.

Genuinely awesome technical and scientific accomplishments as the space shots were, it was the staggering bravery of the men who flew aboard them that captured the public imagination. That "right stuff" never became, even after a decade of suspenseful shots, commonplace. The tense moment at lift-off; the painstaking experiments carried out aloft; the laconic, understated radio reports; the awful stresses of reentry; and not least of all, the strain evident in the families of the crew as they watched on TV with the rest of the nation all added up to a drama that never paled.

American triumphs in space were only a forlorn hope as the decade dawned. News that the Soviets had launched a space satellite, called Sputnik, on October 4, 1957, was galvanic, launching a virtual national state of emotional depression in the U.S.

Not only was the stark fact of Sputnik beeping away out there in space undeniable evidence of Russian scientific and technological superiority—it was downright frightening. What might the Russians *do* with this capability to launch payloads into orbit? Send rockets carrying warheads far around the earth? Establish a military beachhead in deep space? Such were the dark questions raised by Sputnik. A frenzy of self-examination and recrimination swept the country, as people sought to place the blame for being in second place—and to find ways to catch up.

Thus, as the sixties began, the United States not only had to catch up, but had to excel, to achieve a record in space that would reestablish national pride and demonstrate American ability to reach for the stars along with the best of the rest of the world. President John F. Kennedy, with characteristic bluntness, expressed that determination when he asserted that by the end of the decade the United States would send a man to the moon.

The necessary talent and the exotic apparatus were all assembled, and by a superhuman effort the journey at last began. First monkeys went into space—a chimp named Ham in January 1961. Then the first man, Alan Shepard, aboard Mercury-Redstone 3, on May 5, 1961. Then, at last, America sent its first manned orbital mission aloft, and the nation held its breath as John Glenn, on February 20, 1962, circled the planet three times in a dazzling four hours and fifty-four agonizingly suspense-packed minutes. President Kennedy used the occasion to reassert his determination to press on deeper into space. "We have a long way to go in this space race," JFK told John Glenn as he congratulated the astronaut, "but this is the new ocean, and I believe the United States must sail on it and be in a position second to none."

The spacemen beat JFK's moon deadline by five months. The cost was, literally, astronomical: just getting a space vehicle into orbit *around* the moon cost $33 billion. The task was stupendous: three hundred thousand engineers and technical staff, working for no fewer than twenty thousand contractors. The entire science of transistors had to be invented and perfected before the science of computers could reach the necessary development to enable the rocket scientists to plan their launches and recovery. The venture required, too, inestimable courage – "the right stuff" – to climb into the capsule and be blasted into space. Three astronauts, Gus Grissom, Edward White, and Roger Chaffee, gave their lives to the effort in a flash fire in the capsule in 1967.

But, on July 16, 1969, *Apollo 11* roared off the pad, and four days later, earthlings watched Neil Armstrong on TV as he stepped from the capsule onto the gray grit of the moon's surface and declared, "That's one small step for a man, one giant leap for mankind."

The last manned lunar landing took place on December 7, 1972. In the years since, the nation's space scientists and astronauts have concentrated on achieving a dependable space shuttle and space work stations and on sending deep-space probes to explore the farther reaches of the solar system and beyond.

At every step, LIFE reporters and photographers chronicled the adventure. Staffers covered the astronauts and their families under an exclusive contract for their first-person accounts of their epic experiences. LIFE photographer Ralph Morse made covering the astronauts' training a full-time assignment, devising special equipment to capture the drama. To make the full import of the space odyssey meaningful to its readers, LIFE commissioned novelist Norman Mailer to cover a moon shot – and his resultant piece, "Of a Fire on the Moon," became a book in 1970. In it, Mailer tells of a redneck, a man who has trusted machinery all his life, standing gawking up at the giant rocket poised to go, and being baffled and bewildered by it – a powerful image of the common man at the threshold of the space age.

LIFE quoted poet Archibald MacLeish, who said that to see ourselves from the moon "was to see ourselves as riders on the earth together, brothers on that bright loveliness in the eternal cold," and James Dickey, who said about the lunar explorers, in a poem for the magazine's readers, "the secret of time is lying within amazing reach."

*On February 20, 1962, astronaut John Glenn and the Project Mercury capsule* Friendship 7 *lifted off in America's first orbital flight. Glenn circled the earth three times, plunging into three sunsets and three dawns, through four Tuesdays and three Wednesdays – in only five hours.*
1962, Lynn Pelham

*Yury Gagarin, Soviet cosmonaut who on April 12, 1961,
became the first man to orbit the earth, walks a red carpet at
Moscow airport to welcoming ceremonies honoring his flight.
Gagarin, twenty-seven, was in space for one hour forty-eight
minutes. Russians cheered, "Slava Yuri" – "Glory to Yury."*
1961, James Whitmore

*Nearly four thousand people jammed the main concourse of
Grand Central Station in Manhattan to watch John Glenn's
launch on a huge – twelve-by-sixteen-foot – television screen
installed by CBS.*
< 1962, Associated Press

Astronaut Alan Shepard, America's first man in space, is lifted to a helicopter after successfully completing a fifteen-minute suborbital flight. Green dye marks the location of the capsule, which has already been secured to the helicopter for a ride to the recovery ship. Freedom 7, part of Project Mercury, was launched on May 5, 1961.
< 1961, NASA

All the accomplishments of earlier missions had led to a major goal: the rendezvous of two manned spaceships. Gemini 6 and Gemini 7 were chosen, lifting off eleven days apart. For six hours during their flight, the two capsules flew within a few feet of each other, formation flying at 17,500 miles per hour. At the splashdown of Gemini 6, shown here, astronauts Thomas Stafford (left) and Walter Schirra climb out of their capsule. Nearly three days later, Gemini 7 – with Frank Borman and James Lovell aboard – also splashed down safely.
1966, NASA

One objective of America's second manned space project, Gemini, was to enable an astronaut to leave the capsule and move about in space. During the Gemini 4 flight, launched June 3, 1965, Edward White opened the hatch and stepped out, becoming the first American to "walk" in space. He was connected to the capsule by a twenty-four-foot tether that provided him with oxygen and a means of communication. White was so enraptured by the beauty of space he would not end his twenty-minute walk until repeatedly urged to do so by his teammate, James McDivitt.
1965, Major James A. McDivitt

A tracked crawler, the largest land vehicle ever made, and its giant cargo, a Saturn V booster used to blast Apollo capsules into space, dwarf pedestrians at Cape Kennedy. Each three-stage rocket contained eleven engines, developed 7.5 million pounds of thrust at lift-off, and was so tall (364 feet) that it was assembled in a specially constructed building. It was then trucked to one of two launchpads, enabling NASA to schedule a launch every two months.
1966, Yale Joel >

The objective of Project Apollo was to put a three-man space-craft on the moon. This is a photograph of the burned space capsule where the crew of the first Apollo mission — Gus Grissom, Edward White, and Roger Chaffee — tragically lost their lives. They were locked into their positions in the capsule for one of the final systems checkouts when a sudden cry from inside the capsule announced a fire. Technicians worked to open the hatch, battling the flames and fumes pouring from the capsule, but in the five minutes this took, all three men were dead. The disaster put an end to the manned space flights for more than a year and a half, while safer systems were designed.
1967, NASA >

In May 1969, Apollo 10 beamed back the first color television pictures of earth itself. Swirling cloud formations cover part of the earth's surface, but the peninsula of Baja California is easily identifiable, as is part of the North American continent, the brownish mass in the right center of this view.
1969, NASA

Apollo 11 lifts off at the start of one of the greatest trips in history, man's first flight to the moon.
1969, Ralph Morse >

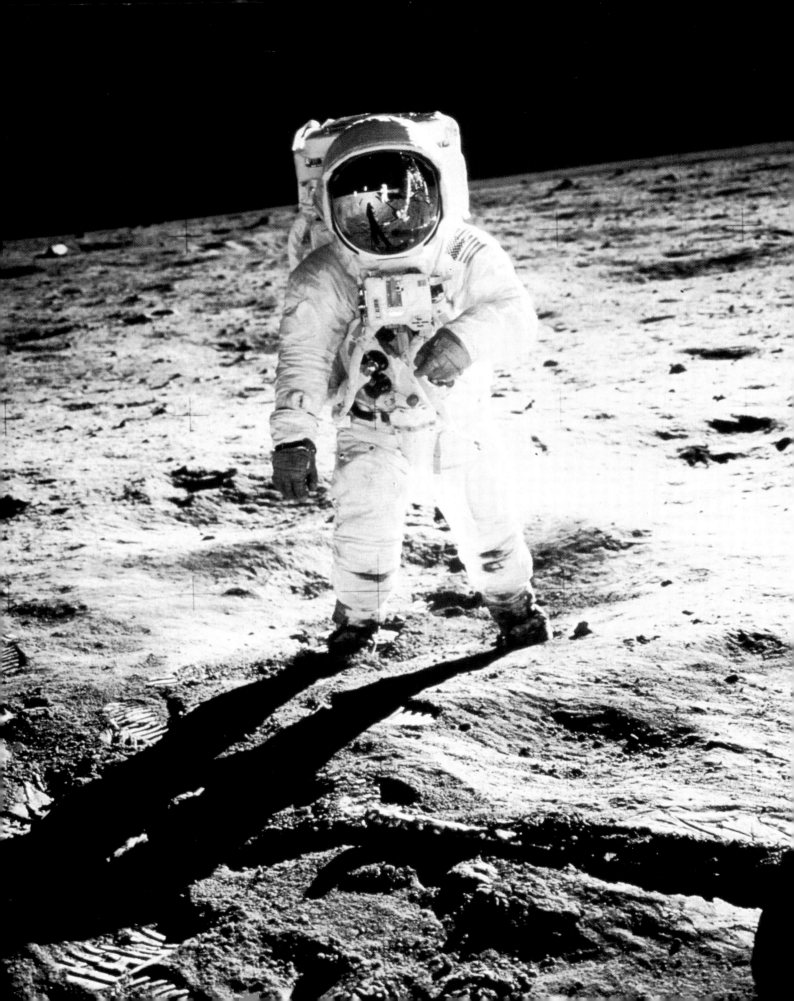

Safe aboard the recovery ship Hornet after their epic flight to
the moon and back, the Apollo 11 team – from left, Armstrong,
Collins, and Aldrin – respond happily from their quarantine
quarters to greetings from the ship's crew.
1969, NASA

A booted foot firmly planted on the lunar surface marks the
successful completion of Apollo 11's earth-to-moon journey.
1969, NASA

On July 20, 1969, Edwin Aldrin followed Neil Armstrong
onto the surface of the moon, where Armstrong took this photograph of him. Reflected in Aldrin's visor are Armstrong,
some scientific equipment, and the lunar module in which
they landed. The Apollo 11 crew members collected rocks and
soil samples and performed experiments and tests for more
than two hours. They then blasted off to rendezvous with
their spacecraft and pilot Michael Collins for the journey
back to planet earth.
< 1969, NASA

# LIFE: The '60s

## 1968

The year 1968 was a paroxysm of rage and violence, grief and anguish around the globe, and at the end, some not-inconsiderable triumph far out in space.

Many Americans spent a good many hours in tears that year as hopes and dreams died amid the echo of yet more bullets from assassins' guns.

In Memphis, Tennessee, on April 3, Dr. Martin Luther King, Jr., leader of America's civil rights movement, told a cheering crowd, "But it doesn't matter with me now....Because I have been to the mountaintop....And I've looked over. And I've seen the promised land. I may not get there with you. But I want you to know tonight, that we, as a people will get to the promised land." The next day, as he stood on a Memphis motel balcony, King, thirty-nine, was shot and killed by a sniper.

On June 5, as he moved through a crowd after a campaign appearance in Los Angeles, Robert Kennedy — jubilant after winning the California and South Dakota primaries — was struck down by two .22-caliber pistol shots. Kennedy, forty-two, died the next day. The killer, a twenty-four-year-old Jordanian immigrant named Sirhan Sirhan, planned the slaying apparently as a reprisal for Kennedy's support of Israel and to mark the anniversary of the Arab defeat in the Six-Day War.

The two murders plunged followers of King and Kennedy into bleak despair — and into rage, as well. Some Kennedy campaign workers found another hero-candidate in Senator Eugene McCarthy; others joined forces with Senator George McGovern. Both ran as liberal democrats; both were ardent opponents of the war in Vietnam. But the killing of King left thousands of his admirers with no such ready outlets for their grief. Distraught blacks took to the streets in violent riots in many cities, including the nation's capital.

Later that summer a King aide, the Reverend Ralph Abernathy, led the Poor People's Campaign to its ramshackle plywood village, Resurrection City, in a month-long encampment on the mall in Washington.

In Czechoslovakia, two hundred thousand soldiers crushed the blossoming of a tentative groping toward freedom. In Paris, students and workers took to the barricades and wielded the traditional weapon of French rebellion — cobblestones — against de Gaulle. They won; he retired.

In Vietnam, where both sides had traditionally observed the lunar new year, called Tet, by ceasing fire, the North Vietnamese this time mounted a savage surprise attack. Enemy thrusts struck at one hundred cities and military posts, including Da Nang and Saigon itself — where the American embassy and the presidential palace were assaulted. In Hue, U.S. troops battled for two months before wresting the city back from the North Vietnamese. At Khe Sanh, Americans were under siege for seventy-six days. Both cities were destroyed. The Tet offensive was a costly one: South Vietnamese and American casualties totaled forty-two hundred dead, sixteen thousand wounded. The Vietcong and North Vietnamese had lost forty-five thousand dead, one hundred thousand wounded, and seven thousand prisoners of war. And militarily, U.S. spokesmen claimed the Tet offensive was a massive defeat for the North Vietnamese. But the enemy had succeeded in shattering home-front confidence in victory. As one U.S. senator, George D. Aiken of Vermont, put it,

"If the Tet offensive was a failure, I hope the Vietcong never have a major success." And the North Vietnamese attacks had demolished President Lyndon Johnson's tenuous popular support for his handling of the war. In the wake of Tet, LBJ stunned the nation by announcing he would not seek reelection. Also, unknown to Americans at home, U.S. troops in March had murdered hundreds of civilians at a village called My Lai. News of the massacre would erupt nineteen months later.

Rising demands by blacks for civil rights, opposition to the Vietnam War, and the growing power of youth in politics had all been on a collision course throughout the decade. They vectored to a cataclysmic eruption on the battleground that was the Democratic national convention in Chicago. The city's cops were braced for the worst: Jeeps festooned with barbed-wire canopies like rolling cheese-slicers were already on standby as delegates arrived. Meanwhile, activists were rolling bandages. What ensued was nothing less, a national investigating panel later decided, than a "police riot." While delegates attended the convention—itself no model of decorum as some black delegates had to fight for their seats, and Mayor Richard Daley was televised calling Senator Abraham Ribicoff a "dirty Jew"—the demonstrators and the police clashed on the streets outside in a fog of tear gas and a hail of billy clubs. Michigan Avenue was lined with troops. The cheese-slicer Jeeps herded demonstrators; those who did not run were bludgeoned by cops.

Hubert Humphrey, his candidacy clear by Lyndon Johnson's withdrawal from the campaign, emerged the Democratic nominee, with Edmund Muskie as his running mate. But Humphrey, distinguished national figure though he was, had badly weakened his popularity among liberals by serving as LBJ's vice president, and he was hardly a clear favorite. Richard Nixon, nominated by the Republicans in Miami to run with Spiro Agnew, was claiming he had a secret plan for handling Vietnam and promising to end the draft and bring the war to a speedy conclusion. Nixon won by more than half a million votes.

But 1968 ended with a historic—and successful—adventure deep in space. On December 21, astronauts Frank Borman, James Lovell, and William Anders rode a Saturn V booster into space and then blasted off for the moon aboard *Apollo 8*. They achieved the first manned orbit of earth's mysterious satellite, completing eight lunar orbits. On Christmas Eve, the three took turns reading from the Bible's Book of Genesis over the radio as they orbited the moon. "And God called the dry land Earth; and the gathering together of the waters He called Seas; and God saw that it was good," Mission Commander Borman read to the folks back on earth. The next day, the three set off for the return voyage. A friend telegraphed Borman upon his triumphant arrival: "You have bailed out 1968!"

"I shall not seek, and I will not accept, the nomination of my party for another term as your President." With that unequivocal assertion, Lyndon Baines Johnson stunned the nation in a historic TV address that threw the 1968 Democratic race wide open.
1968, Alfred Eisenstaedt

Protesting students take over the office of the president of Columbia University. After six days of campus unrest and the occupation of five buildings, the students were evicted by a force of one thousand New York City policemen. While the demonstrators' methods were sharply criticized, an investigation led to the resignation of the president, Grayson Kirk.
1968, Gerald S. Upham >

Martin Luther King, Jr., had gone to Memphis, Tennessee, in April 1968 to help organize marches by the city's sanitation men, most of whom were black. One evening before dinner, as he talked with friends on the balcony of his motel, a rifle was fired from a rooming house across the street. Here Dr. King lies mortally wounded, while friends point in the direction from which the shot had come. The assailant escaped, but eleven months later James Earl Ray, a white drifter and escaped convict, confessed to the crime and was sentenced to ninety-nine years in prison. Many suspected that Ray was paid to kill King, but this has never been proved.
1968. Joseph Louw

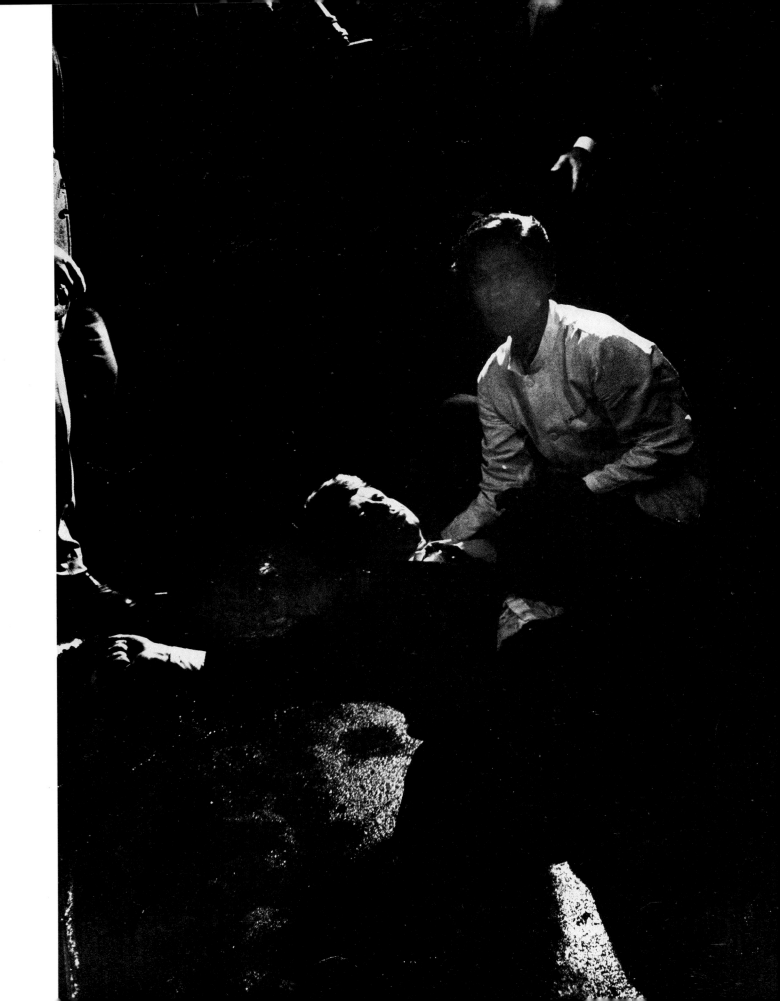

The night of the 1968 California presidential primary, the
Kennedy party gathered in Los Angeles at the Ambassador
Hotel to await the returns – and to celebrate winning. Senator
Robert Kennedy gave his victory speech to loyal campaign
workers and, on his way to meet with the press, took a short-
cut through the hotel's kitchen area. Waiting for him there
was a Jordanian fanatic, Sirhan Sirhan. Armed with a .22
pistol, Sirhan shot Kennedy twice in the head. Here Kennedy
lies dying on the concrete floor. Juan Romero, a busboy whose
hand Kennedy had stopped to shake only a moment before,
tries to comfort him.

< 1968, Bill Eppridge

Children display an American flag and sadly wave farewell
as a special train bearing Senator Robert Kennedy's casket
and his family and friends travels south to Washington, D.C.
After Kennedy's morning funeral in St. Patrick's Cathedral
in New York City, he was buried that night in Arlington
National Cemetery, not far from the grave of his brother
John F. Kennedy.

1968, Bill Eppridge

Regional rivalries that had troubled Nigeria for many years
were greatly aggravated when the eastern part of the country,
Biafra, broke away in May 1967. Nigerian troops encircled
Biafra and blockaded its ports. Thousands of isolated Bia-
frans were starving but refused to accept relief shipments that
came through the Nigerian government, suspecting that such
food had been poisoned. While these and thousands of other
Biafran children were starving, tons of supplies rotted in
Nigerian stockpiles across the battle lines. Finally, in January
1970, Biafra – on the verge of total collapse – ceased to exist
as an independent nation.
1970, Romano Cagnoni

*Too weak to play, emaciated Biafran children await death
from kwashiorkor, protein starvation, at a camp of refugees
near Aba. "Like an anteroom to Hell," reported LIFE of the
camps in Biafra. Kwashiorkor had killed more people in the
first eighteen months of the civil war than died in the pre-
vious seven years of fighting in Vietnam. Families of some of
these children were killed in the shelling and air raids of the
war with the Nigerians; others were abandoned.*
1968, Hubert Le Campion

Fear that the growing sense of freedom enjoyed by the Czech people in the summer of 1968 might spread to other East European countries appears to have been the motive for the sudden Soviet invasion of the country. Without warning, Russian T-62 tanks were in the streets of Liberec, shown here, and Prague early on the morning of August 21, 1968. Buildings were destroyed, people threatened, their leaders arrested, and the spirit of freedom was completely snuffed out.
1968, Ivan Simon

Urged by their government to show no resistance, Czech citizens could show only their flag and fight back with sticks, stones, jeers, and firebombs in a courageous display of defiance against the Soviet invasion.
1968, Hilmar Pabel >

*Tommie Smith (center) and John Carlos (right) raise black-gloved fists during the playing of "The Star Spangled Banner" at the 1968 Olympic Games in Mexico City. This gesture was intended as a show of protest against racism in the U.S.*
1968, John Dominis

*Student unrest boiled into the streets of Paris, where it turned into a bloody confrontation with police. At issue was student discontent with the university system and disapproval of what they saw as France's embrace of modernity at the expense of humanistic ideals.*
< 1968, Jean-Pierre Rey

Demonstrations against the Vietnam War had been erupting across the country with increasing frequency. They reached new records for ugliness and violence during the four days of the Democratic national convention in Chicago in August. Here, protesters taunt the police with shouts and obscene gestures. The police lost control and responded with vicious physical force.
1968, Perry C. Riddle, *The Chicago Daily News*

Even some of the press got slugged around by the Chicago police at the convention. Here a bandaged NBC reporter interviews another casualty.
1968, *The Chicago Sun-Times* >

During the Democratic convention, Chicago police and antiwar forces do battle on Michigan Avenue. The protesters, determined to reach the convention headquarters, broke through the police and National Guard lines. Police used rifle butts, fists, feet, tear gas, and clubs in savage battle with the demonstrators. Much of this violence was seen by TV audiences in the U.S. and overseas, and it drew widespread condemnation.
1968, UPI/Bettmann Newsphotos

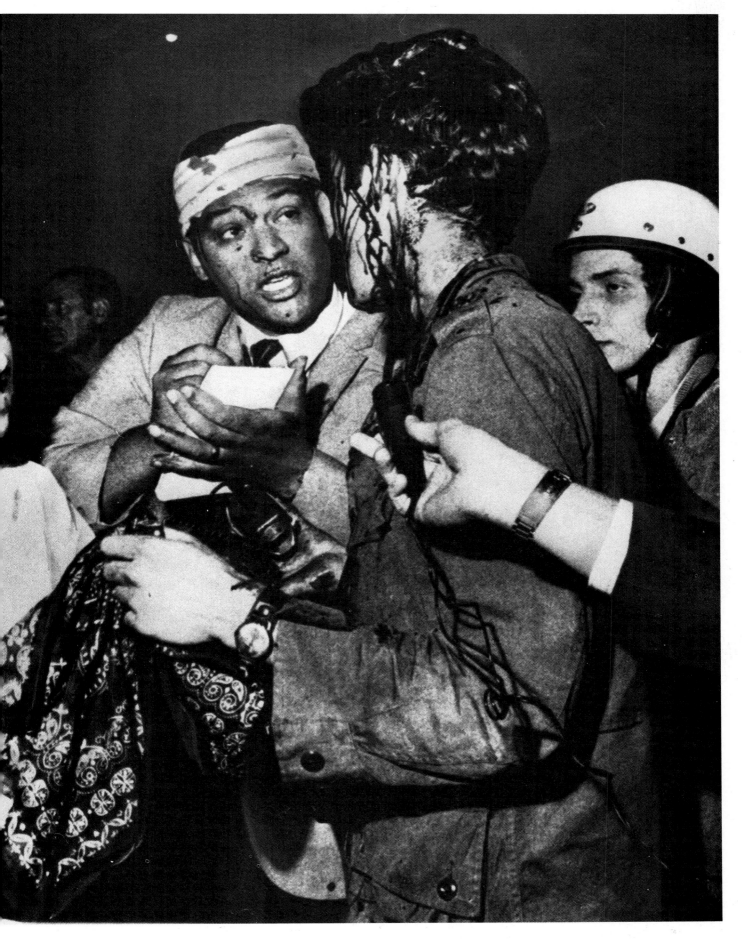

*With son-in-law David Eisenhower, daughters Julie Eisenhower and Tricia, and his wife, Pat, Richard M. Nixon thrusts two triumphant V's for victory skyward after learning he has defeated Hubert Humphrey for the presidency.*
1968, Bob Peterson

## Vietnam

If one nation in Southeast Asia fell to the Communists, the logic behind the U.S. involvement in Vietnam went, the others would fall like so many dominoes. As Dwight David Eisenhower put it on April 7, 1954, "You knock over the first one, and the last one will go over very quickly."

By the time Eisenhower left office, the United States, continuing assistance begun under President Harry Truman, had some two thousand military "advisers" in South Vietnam to guide the army of that tiny embattled nation in protecting itself—and thus safeguard the region for the interests of democracy.

American intervention in Vietnam ignored a long history of a similar effort by the French that was rich in some crucial facts about the enemy and the awful nature of the leech-ridden jungle terrain. The North Vietnamese had a fierce and dogged willingness to fight a guerrilla war, and the jungle, with its thick canopy of foliage and razor-sharp elephant grass, gave him an ideal arena in which to fight it—and to hide after he had struck.

After World War II, the French had tried to regain control of their former colony, only to meet stiff nationalist resistance under the direction of Ho Chi Minh which culminated in the slaughtering of the French troops at Dien Bien Phu in 1954.

Soon after, a Geneva agreement partitioned the country at the seventeenth parallel of latitude, with a demilitarized zone (DMZ) on either side. Ho was to govern Vietnam to the north, and a new government was to rule the south—but for only two years, after which national elections would determine the future government. It was, of course, a formula for disaster. Catholic refugees fleeing communism poured south; Ho's guerrillas began infiltrating. The shaky government of Ngo Dinh Diem in South Vietnam began to get aid from the United States—the U.S. government was still anxious to see that this domino did not fall, despite the lack of true democracy in the south. Buddhist monks, for example, set themselves afire to protest Diem's harsh discrimination against their religion.

Soon after Lyndon Johnson became commander in chief, the facade of merely advising in the war evaporated as the result of a naval encounter in the Gulf of Tonkin. In it, U.S. vessels reported they had been attacked by North Vietnamese gunboats. LBJ directed bombings of North Vietnamese harbors and asked Congress for—and on August 7, 1964, got—authorization "to take all necessary steps, including the use of armed force, to assist" South Vietnam.

The war against Ho's rebels turned into a quagmire that devoured money and men. Into it the U.S. government poured both, with nothing to show for it, year after year, except a mounting casualty toll. Public awareness of the ugly little war began to grow as U.S. troop commitments—and casualties—mounted. Draft laws excused college students, resulting in a heavily blue-collar and largely black military. To try to limit the casualties and the increasingly noisy protests against the war, the U.S. began "Operation Rolling Thunder," aerial attacks on the north.

But despite the mounting U.S. force, against crack Green Beret operations, against napalm strikes, and against all the rest of the massed technology of helicopters and defoliants, the Vietcong continued his guerrilla war. American soldiers found themselves in a war where a bicycle could contain a bomb; where a rice paddy could be full of sharpened, poisoned bamboo stakes called punji sticks; where children and old women could be the enemy. This confusion led to instances of killing innocent civilians.

Additional atrocities occurred, the most notorious being the massacre of the villagers of My Lai by members of Lieutenant William Calley's platoon. On March 16, 1968, the U.S. soldiers murdered hundreds of unarmed Vietnamese, including women and children.

Top officials had been optimistic at the outset of the war. Defense Secretary McNamara, for example, came back to Washington from a visit to headquarters in Saigon in 1964 and said U.S. troops could begin withdrawal the following year. He was not reckoning with the determination of the North Vietnamese. "How long do you Americans want to fight?" North Vietnam's premier, Pham Van Dong, asked *New York Times* reporter Harrison Salisbury in 1966. "One year? Two years? Three years? Five years? Ten years? Twenty years? We will be glad to accommodate you." By early 1968, McNamara was reported in tears as he described the futility of having dropped more bombs on Vietnam than had been dropped on all of Europe in World War II — and shortly afterward, Johnson announced McNamara's departure for the World Bank.

If the war was hellish to fight and impossible to manage, it was easy to cover — some correspondents simply commuted to the fighting by helicopter — but incredibly difficult and dangerous to cover well. Some forty-five journalists died covering Vietnam, including LIFE photographer Larry Burrows, killed when his helicopter was shot down over Laos.

The Tet offensive had been a major turning point in American support, not so much for the war, but for the administration's management of it. After Ho sent his troops surging against the cities and military installations of the south, penetrating even into the U.S. embassy in Saigon, many Americans wondered, as did CBS anchorman Walter Cronkite as he read the news ticker, "What the hell's going on? I thought we were winning this war." TV news coverage brought the savagery and the horror of the combat into living rooms as Americans watched twenty-one American and South Vietnamese battalions fight for almost six weeks to take the city of Hue back from eight North Vietnamese battalions. In the six weeks following the Tet offensive, public approval of LBJ's generalship dropped from 40 percent to just 26 percent.

By opting in 1968 not to run again, Johnson could — and did — rid himself of the Vietnam dilemma. It took the rest of the U.S. a bit longer to disengage.

But thirty years after the first U.S. casualty — an Office of Strategic Services agent killed in 1945 — and after 57,605 more Americans had been killed and 303,700 more wounded, 766 taken prisoner, 5,011 declared missing, and some $165 billion spent on the war, the United States did clear out, leaving South Vietnam in April of 1975. Even then, however, the war had not ended for many U.S. servicemen. They returned, not as conquering heroes, to a nation that did not understand why they had fought. Many were — and still are — suffering from delayed stress syndrome as a result of the unique horrors of the war in Vietnam.

The North Vietnamese, who had lost 444,000 dead soldiers and 587,000 civilians killed, took over shortly afterward.

South Vietnamese soldiers herd tautly bound
Vietcong and a wicker sack full of documents
into a peasant's canoe for the trip to headquarters and prison.
1962, Larry Burrows

U.S. advisers to the South Vietnamese army
survey its performance: Vietcong soldiers,
shot down on the delta, lie dead while their
captured comrades huddle nearby.
1962, Larry Burrows

Americans were at the controls, and manning the machine
guns at the doors, as these H-21 helicopters ferried South
Vietnamese troops into surprise attack against the Vietcong.
< 1964, Larry Burrows

On a Saigon street, an elderly Buddhist monk named Quang Duc immolates himself as a protest against the years of religious persecution that Buddhists, a majority of the South Vitenamese population, had suffered under the pro-Catholic government of Ngo Dinh Diem. Other Buddhist suicides followed Quang Duc's, leading to the eventual collapse of the government and the assassination of President Diem.
1963, Associated Press

A terrified Vietcong kneels in supplication before a bayonet-wielding South Vietnamese soldier demanding to know where arms are buried. When the prisoner refused to talk, the guard let him go — to a prison camp — unharmed. Both sides in the war occasionally used torture.
1962, Larry Burrows >

Saigon volunteers desperately fight an explosion and fire in a South Vietnamese army ordnance installation.
1965, Burke Uzzle

A South Vietnamese family is reunited after a savage two-day battle for their village of Dong Xoai. Their faces reflect anguish as they realize how many have been killed.
1965, Horst Faas for Associated Press

A pro-Ky government soldier takes the shoes off the feet of a rebel soldier captured and executed on the spot during a battle in the rebellion of Buddhist-led troops in Da Nang, South Vietnam.
1966, UPI/Bettmann Newsphotos

Private First Class Thomas Cole, a wounded medic with the 1st Cavalry Division, attends a seriously wounded comrade, Staff Sergeant Harrison Pell, during the struggle for control of the central highlands of South Vietnam. This photograph won the Overseas Press Club Award for "superlative still photography requiring exceptional courage."
1966, Henri Huet for Associated Press >>

A Vietcong prisoner is held under close guard. His eyes and mouth are taped so that he cannot communicate with his comrades as he is taken back to a prisoner-of-war compound.
1965, Paul Schutzer >>>

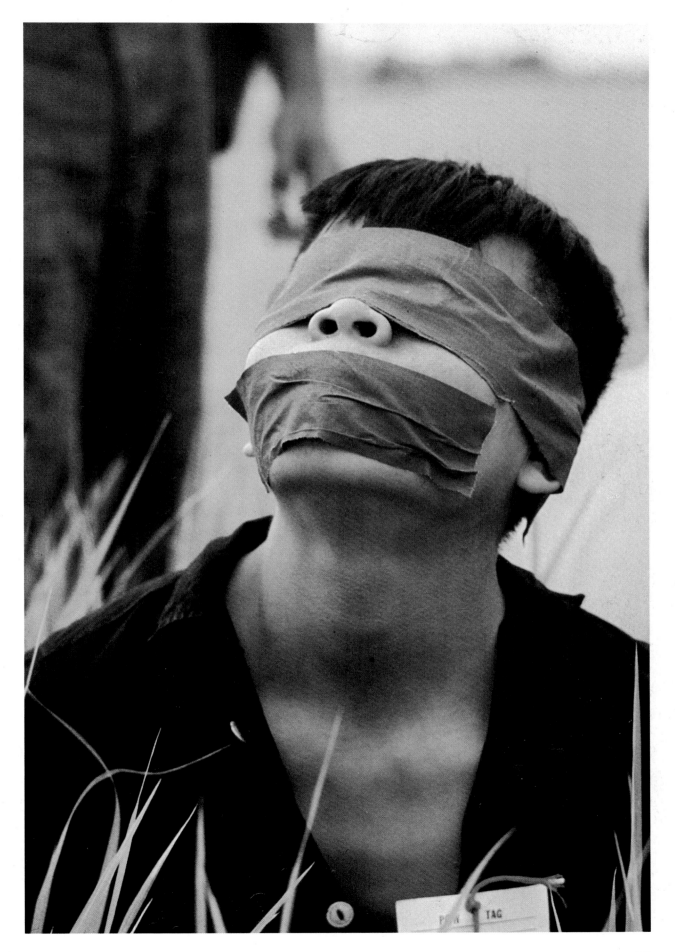

*The World War II C-47, refitted with three multibarreled machine guns, proved itself again twenty years later in Vietnam. Redesignated the AC-47 and called the Dragonship, it could bank up to sixty degrees and fire eighteen thousand rounds a minute. This photograph was taken from the open doorway of one of these Puffs, which were nicknamed after the song "Puff the Magic Dragon."*
1966, Larry Burrows

Private First Class Phillip Wilson carries a rocket launcher across a stream in the demilitarized zone, the DMZ. He was killed in action a few days later. The five-mile-wide DMZ was established between North and South Vietnam as an area where no military action was to be permitted. But starting in May 1966, U.S. aerial photographs of the zone revealed enemy troops swarming into South Vietnam. Counterattack meant long, fierce, and bloody fighting through mountain and jungle terrain as difficult as any the marines had ever seen. This photograph and the three following were taken during the action there.

1966, Larry Burrows

Hurt during the fighting to halt enemy invasions southward through the demilitarized zone, a young marine – his blank stare indicating he is in shock – is tended to by a buddy.
1966, Larry Burrows

Wounded in the head and knee in a firefight near Hill 484, a marine reaches out to a stricken comrade at a muddy, make-shift hilltop first-aid station.
1966, Larry Burrows >>

Four marines recover the body of a comrade as their company comes under fire. The photographer at right is a twenty-one-year-old Parisian, Catherine LeRoy, one of the few women who covered the Vietnam War.
< 1966, Larry Burrows

*Lieutenant Commander Richard A. Stratton, a U.S. fighter pilot shot down over North Vietnam and held prisoner for more than six years, obeys his captor's command to bow at a televised news conference in Hanoi, after his "confession" had been read.*
1967, Lee Lockwood from Black Star

*During an air raid alert, residents of Hanoi wait in chest-deep sidewalk shelters for the all-clear signal. This photo was taken by the first American photographer since 1954 permitted to report on daily life in the capital of North Vietnam.*
1967, Lee Lockwood from Black Star

*A marine at the siege of Con Thien – "Hill of Angels" in Vietnamese – pauses during a long and intense battle. The Vietcong had mounted its heaviest artillery attack, and the U.S. countered with even greater force.*
1967, David Douglas Duncan >

*A suspected Vietcong terrorist, whose hands were tied behind his back, was shot in the head by National Police Chief Brigadier General Nguyen Ngoc Loan. The execution took place during the Tet offensive, when the Vietcong invaded Saigon. This photograph received a Pulitzer Prize in 1969.*
< 1968, Eddie Adams

On March 16, 1968, Lieutenant William L. Calley, Jr., arrived in the South Vietnamese village of My Lai in pursuit of Vietcong militia. He directed the twenty-five men of his Company C platoon to round up the civilians of My Lai and drive them into a ravine. The unarmed villagers, estimated at more than one hundred in number, were then slaughtered by the Americans. Throughout the rest of the day the soldiers continued killing hundreds more, including women and children, and committed other atrocities. The bodies shown here, photographed on the day of the massacre, were found on the road leading from the village. A U.S. Army court-martial was held in 1971. Of the many officers and enlisted men accused, only Lieutenant Calley was convicted. His ultimate punishment was three years of house arrest at Fort Benning, Georgia.
1968, Ronald L. Haeberle

*Marines load their dead onto a helicopter for the trip home from Khe Sanh.*
< 1968, David Douglas Duncan

A paratrooper of the 101st Airborne Division guides a medical evacuation helicopter into a jungle clearing west of Hue. The casualties occurred while the unit was on a five-day patrol of an area held by the Vietcong.
1968, Art Greenspon for Associated Press

In April 1968 General Westmoreland ordered the 1st Air Cavalry to relieve the marines at the U.S. outpost in Khe Sanh, which had been cut off by North Vietnamese in January. Fleets of helicopters lifted men and artillery into the rugged hills, and after a week of intense fighting the two forces joined, ending the eleven-week siege.
1968, Larry Burrows

*Returning from the front lines of the battle to recapture Hue, one of many Vietnamese cities attacked during the Tet offensive, a tank converted into an ambulance carries badly wounded marines.*
1968, John Olson

*During the 1968 Tet offensive, when the Vietcong occupied Hue, residents – soldiers, women, and children – were marched into open pits, where they were shot or clubbed to death. The mass graves were discovered a year later, and the bodies were laid out to be identified. Here a woman grieves over her husband's remains.*
1969, Larry Burrows

*In a dramatic moment that vividly symbolized the antiwar movement, one young civilian stepped forward and put carnations down the rifle barrels aimed at him during a demonstration in Washington, D.C., in October 1967.*

1967, Bernie Boston

*Flower power blossoms as advocates practice just being — and, not just incidentally, they catch some rays, too — at the big Central Park Be-in.*
1969, Steve Schapiro

# 1960

**World:** Russians shoot down U.S. spy plane, U-2 pilot Gary Powers captured / Khrushchev at UN denounces U.S. policies / Israeli agents seize Adolf Eichmann in Argentina / Chaos in Congo Republic leads to UN intervention / South African blacks, marching to protest new law requiring passes at all times, massacred in Sharpeville / Castro confiscates U.S. property / Guatemala joins Nicaragua in accusing Castro of fomenting uprisings, Ike sends naval units to patrol region / South Vietnam's Ngo Dinh Diem regains power after coup, dissidents organize as Vietcong / South Korea's Syngman Rhee orders martial law as students protest rigged elections, National Assembly calls for new balloting, Rhee flees country.

**U.S.A.:** Kennedy, Johnson win narrow presidential victory / Civil rights issues create turmoil in South / Congress investigates "payola" in recording, broadcasting industries; underworld influence in pro boxing; teamsters union.

**Firsts:** Pacemakers / Communications, weather satellites / Felt-tip pen / Laser / Quasars observed.

**Movies:** Psycho / The Apartment / Elmer Gantry / The Entertainer / Inherit the Wind / Exodus / Tunes of Glory / Hiroshima, Mon Amour / Never on Sunday / Big Deal on Madonna Street / Our Man in Havana / Butterfield Eight / Sunrise at Campobello / Please Don't Eat the Daisies / Spartacus / Suddenly Last Summer / The World of Suzie Wong / The Alamo / The Dark at the Top of the Stairs / G.I. Blues / Can-Can.

**Songs:** Are You Lonesome Tonight? / Camelot / Everybody's Somebody's Fool / Hey, Look Me Over / Lollipops and Roses / Green Fields / Itsy Bitsy, Teenie Weenie, Yellow Polka-Dot Bikini / Mr. Lucky / What's the Matter with Kids Today? / The Twist / How to Handle a Woman / If Ever I Would Leave You / Blue Angel / Partin' Time.

**Stage:** Toys in the Attic / A Thurber Carnival / A Taste of Honey / Advise and Consent / Becket / Camelot / Irma La Douce / Wildcat / The Unsinkable Mollie Brown / Bye Bye Birdie.

**Books:** To Kill a Mockingbird (Lee) / Born Free (Adamson) / This Is My God (Wouk) / The Leopard (Di Lampedusa) / The Chapman Report (Wallace) / Rabbit, Run (Updike) / The Sotweed Factor (Barth) / Welcome to Hard Times (Doctorow) / The Rise and Fall of the Third Reich (Shirer).

**TV in the '60s:** Gunsmoke (Premiere '55) / Have Gun Will Travel ('57) / Wagon Train ('57) / Andy Griffith ('60) / The Real McCoys ('57) / Rawhide ('59) / Candid Camera ('48) / The Untouchables ('59) / The Price Is Right ('56) / Jack Benny ('50) / Bonanza ('59) / Hazel ('61) / Perry Mason ('57) / Red Skelton ('53) / Danny Thomas ('53) / Dr. Kildare ('61) / Dennis the Menace ('59) / My Three Sons ('60) / 77 Sunset Strip ('58) / Ed Sullivan ('48) / Alfred Hitchcock ('55) / Lassie ('54) / What's My Line? ('50) / Jackie Gleason ('52) / Garry Moore ('58) / Dick Van Dyke ('61) / My Favorite Martian ('63) / Donna Reed ('58) / Bewitched ('64) / Gomer Pyle ('64) / The Fugitive ('63) / Peyton Place ('64) / Walt Disney ('54) / The Beverly Hillbillies ('62) / The Lucy Show ('62) / Ben Casey ('61) / Father Knows Best ('54) / Petticoat Junction ('63) / The Munsters ('64) / Gilligan's Island ('64) / Get Smart ('65) / The Man from U.N.C.L.E. ('64) / Lawrence Welk ('55) / The FBI ('65) / Mission: Impossible ('66) / Dean Martin ('65) The Smothers Brothers Comedy Hour ('67) / Carol Burnett ('67) / Mayberry R.F.D. ('68) / Julia ('68) / Here's Lucy ('68) / Glen Campbell ('69) / Hawaii Five-O ('68) / Family Affair ('66).

# 1961

**World:** U.S. breaks diplomatic ties with Cuba, Bay of Pigs invasion fails / East Germany builds Berlin Wall / UN secretary general Hammarskjöld dies in plane crash / JFK increases U.S. advisers in South Vietnam / Angolans rebel against Portuguese rule / South Africa leaves British Commonwealth, incurs UN censure for apartheid / Pope John XXIII issues encyclical (*Mater et Magistra*) condemning materialism, birth control / Chou En-lai walks out on Moscow party congress, heralding Sino-Soviet break.

**U.S.A.:** In farewell address, Ike warns nation of danger in military-industrial complex / JFK inaugurated / Peace Corps established / Alabama mobs attack Freedom Riders protesting bus segregation / Ernest Hemingway dies of self-inflicted gunshot / Malcolm X advocates black power, racial separation / New York Yankee Roger Maris hits sixty-one homers / Widespread point-shaving in college basketball.

**Firsts:** Man in orbit (Gagarin) / Genetic code broken / U.S. suborbital flight (Shepard) / Televised presidential news conference / Nonstop two-way English Channel swim (Abertando) / Nondairy creamer.

**Movies:** The Hustler / A Raisin in the Sun / Splendor in the Grass / El Cid / Judgment at Nuremberg / One, Two, Three / The Misfits / The Absent-Minded Professor / The Guns of Navarone / Misty / Breakfast at Tiffany's / Summer and Smoke / Breathless / La Dolce Vita / Two Women / West Side Story / Fanny / Babes in Toyland / Flower Drum Song / Wild in the Country.

**Songs:** Moon River / Where the Boys Are / Big Bad John / The Bilbao Song / I Believe in You / Michael — Row the Boat Ashore / Travelin' Man / Yellow Bird / Happy Birthday, Sweet Sixteen / I'm a Woman / Baby, You're Right / Kiss Me Quick / Can't Help Falling in Love / The Fly / Hit the Road, Jack / Little Sister / Barbara Ann.

**Stage:** Come Blow Your Horn / Rhinoceros / Mary, Mary / Purlie Victorious / The Caretaker / A Shot in the Dark / Take Her, She's Mine / The Night of the Iguana / A Man for All Seasons / Ross / The Blacks / How to Succeed in Business Without Really Trying / Subways Are for Sleeping / Milk and Honey.

**Books:** The Agony and the Ecstasy (Stone) / Franny and Zooey (Salinger) / The Carpetbaggers (Robbins) / Daughter of Silence (West) / The Making of the President, 1960 (White) / A Nation of Sheep (Lederer) / Ring of Bright Water (Maxwell) / Shadows on the Grass (Dinesen) / Nobody Knows My Name (Baldwin) / The White Nile (Moorehead) / Fate Is the Hunter (Gann) / Catch-22 (Heller) / A Burnt-Out Case (Greene) / The Moviegoer (Percy).

**Fads:** Yo-yos / Rocking chairs / Surfboarding / The Jackie Kennedy look / Bed-pushing / Decorated sneakers.

## 1962

**World:** U.S.S.R. frees pilot Gary Powers in exchange for spy Rudolf Abel / Algeria wins independence from France / UN troops quell Congo Republic civil war / Castro releases 1,113 Bay of Pigs POWs for $53 million in food, medical supplies / Soviet missile bases in Cuba discovered, U.S. quarantine forces Khrushchev to dismantle them / U.S. creates military assistance command in South Vietnam / Pathet Lao takes over northern Laos / Thailand coalition under Premier Souvanna Phouma supported by Britain, Australia, U.S. / Pope John XXIII opens Twenty-first Ecumenical Council (Vatican II).

**U.S.A.:** Supreme Court rules scheduled recitation of school prayers unconstitutional / Black student James Meredith seeks to enroll at U. of Mississippi, U.S. troops move in to control campus riots / Richard Nixon quits politics after defeat in California gubernatorial race / Government bans segregation in housing, military reserves, transportation / Freedom rides continue / Marilyn Monroe dies in Los Angeles, apparent suicide.

**Firsts:** Nuclear warhead fired from sub (*Polaris*) / City-owned TV station (WNYC, New York) / Synthetic wigs (Dynel) / Underwater Channel swim (Baldasare, using Aqua-lung).

**Movies:** Advise and Consent / Long Day's Journey into Night / Billy Budd / Birdman of Alcatraz / The Longest Day / The Children's Hour / Freud / Light in the Piazza / Lawrence of Arabia / Lolita / The Manchurian Candidate / Sergeants Three / Sweet Bird of Youth / To Kill a Mockingbird / Walk on the Wild Side / What Ever Happened to Baby Jane? / The Music Man / Gypsy / Divorce – Italian Style / A Taste of Honey / Sundays and Cybele.

**Songs:** I Can't Stop Loving You / Roses Are Red / Blowin' in the Wind / Ramblin' Rose / Days of Wine and Roses / Any Day Now / The Girl from Ipanema / Breaking Up Is Hard to Do / Desafinado / Call Me Mr. In-Between / That Happy Feeling / Quiet Nights of Quiet Stars / Second Hand Love / The Wah-Watusi / Mashed Potato Time / Let Me In / Twistin' the Night Away / He's a Rebel / Lonely Teardrops.

**Stage:** A Thousand Clowns / Who's Afraid of Virginia Woolf? / Never Too Late / Oh Dad, Poor Dad, Mama's Hung You in the Closet and I'm Feeling So Sad / Seidman and Son / Beyond the Fringe / I Can Get It for You Wholesale / No Strings / Little Me / A Funny Thing Happened on the Way to the Forum.

**Books:** Another Country (Baldwin) / Ship of Fools (Porter) / Pale Fire (Nabokov) / A Long and Happy Life (Price) / The Thin Red Line (Jones) / Letting Go (Roth) / The Reivers (Faulkner) / Youngblood Hawke (Wouk) / Tropic of Capricorn (Miller) / Silent Spring (Carson) / One Flew Over the Cuckoo's Nest (Kesey) / Big Sur (Kerouac).

**Fads:** "Twist" (fringed) apparel / The Cleopatra look / *Last Year in Marienbad* hairdos / Intercollegiate tiddledywinks.

## 1963

**World:** U.S.S.R., Britain, U.S. ban nuclear tests in atmosphere, space, underwater / British war secretary Profumo resigns in sex-tinged spy scandal / Kim Philby of British Intelligence defects to Russia, revealed as third man in 1951 Burgess-Maclean spy case / Major earthquake rocks Yugoslavia / Italian dam collapses, wave drowns 1,800 / Ghanaian students in Bulgaria, U.S.S.R. charge hosts with racial bias / Kenya wins independence / Hurricane Flora slams into Haiti, 2,500 perish / Buddhist priests, nuns in South Vietnam immolate selves to protest policies of Diem regime, Diem assassinated after military coup / Indonesia's Sukarno becomes president for life.

**U.S.A.:** NAACP's Medgar Evers shot to death in Jackson, Mississippi / Informer Joseph Valachi identifies organized crime bosses to Senate committee / Texas financier Billie Sol Estes convicted of huge fraud / Dr. Martin Luther King, Jr., leads March on Washington to push equal rights for blacks / President Kennedy slain in Dallas, Lyndon Johnson sworn in, Chief Justice Warren heads panel to investigate assassination.

**Firsts:** Use of artificial heart in operation (DeBakey) / U.S.-born person beatified (Mother Seton) / Polaroid color film / State lottery (New Hampshire).

**Movies:** Heavens Above! / Hud / Cleopatra / 8½ / Tom Jones / The L-Shaped Room / The Leopard / Lilies of the Field / The Birds / The Ugly American / Dr. No / The Great Escape / Lord of the Flies / Knife in the Water / David and Lisa / Love with the Proper Stranger / Charade / The Cardinal / The Condemned of Altona / Under the Yum-Yum Tree.

**Songs:** All My Loving / Call Me Irresponsible / Charade / Dominique / Guantanamera / Hellow Muddah, Hello Fadduh / He's So Fine / Blue Velvet / Go Away, Little Girl / Our Day Will Come / If I Had a Hammer / More / Puff the Magic Dragon / Wives and Lovers / Ballad of Hollis Brown / As Long As He Needs Me / Detroit City.

**Stage:** Barefoot in the Park / The Milk Train Doesn't Stop Here Anymore / Photo Finish / Enter Laughing / Luther / The Ballad of the Sad Café / Rattle of a Simple Man / Tovarich / 110 in the Shade / Oliver! / She Loves Me.

**Books:** The Group (McCarthy) / The Centaur (Updike) / Caravans (Michener) / The Sand Pebbles (McKenna) / V. (Pynchon) / Cat's Cradle (Vonnegut) / Powers of Attorney (Auchincloss) / A Singular Man (Donleavy) / The Fire Next Time (Baldwin) / The Feminine Mystique (Friedan) / The American Way of Death (Mitford) / What Is Remembered (Toklas) / Beyond the Melting Pot (Glazer, Moynihan)

**Fads:** Piano-wrecking / Teen party crashing in gangs / The Bardot bowler (hat) / Sweater for two (two necks, two sleeves).

## 1964

**World:** Khrushchev deposed / Harold Wilson becomes Britain's prime minister / Microphones found in walls of U.S. Moscow embassy / Catholic Ecumenical Council exonerates Jews of guilt in Crucifixion / Saudi Arabia's King Ibn Saud sacked, Faisal takes over / Malta, Malawi, Zambia achieve independence / PLO organized / Eight South African black leaders given life sentences / Twenty-one Panamanians, four GIs killed in Canal Zone riots / Brazil's military revolts, anti-Communist purge follows / Bolivia's government falls in military coup / Red China announces it has A-bomb / India's Nehru dies / North Vietnamese attack U.S. destroyers in Gulf of Tonkin, Congress authorizes President to "prevent further aggression."

**U.S.A.:** Johnson, Humphrey win big / Civil rights law enacted / Teamsters' Jimmy Hoffa convicted of fraud, jury tampering / Malcolm X forms Black Nationalist party / Demonstrations protesting deepening involvement in South Vietnam spread / Surgeon general's report links smoking to lung cancer, other diseases / Elizabeth Taylor marries Richard Burton.

**Firsts:** Nuclear-powered lighthouse (Chesapeake Bay) / Methadone therapy for heroin addicts / In-flight movies.

**Movies:** Becket / Yesterday, Today and Tomorrow / The Pink Panther / From Russia with Love / The Night of the Iguana / A Hard Day's Night / Fail Safe / Topkapi / Mary Poppins / My Fair Lady / The Americanization of Emily / Zorba the Greek / Marriage Italian Style / Goldfinger / The Prize / Dr. Strangelove / Seven Days in May / What a Way to Go! / Black Like Me.

**Songs:** Chim Chim Cher-ee / A Spoonful of Sugar / And I Love Her / Can't Buy Me Love / A Hard Day's Night / I Want to Hold Your Hand / Love Me Do / Baby Love / Dang Me / Don't Rain on My Parade / Downtown / Everybody Loves Somebody / Goin' Out of My Head / Goldfinger / Hello, Dolly! / If I Ruled the World / If I Were a Rich Man / King of the Road / Leader of the Pack / Matchmaker, Matchmaker / Mr. Tambourine Man / My Kind of Town / Oh, Pretty Woman / People / Pink Panther Theme / Sunrise, Sunset / Walk on By / We'll Sing in the Sunshine / Who Can I Turn To.

**Stage:** After the Fall / Any Wednesday / The Subject Was Roses / The Deputy / What Makes Sammy Run? / Luv / Hello, Dolly! / Fiddler on the Roof / Funny Girl.

**Books:** Herzog (Bellow) / Candy (Southern, Hoffenberg) / Armageddon (Uris) / The Rector of Justin (Auchincloss) / You Only Live Twice (Fleming) / Convention (Knebel, Bailey) / Reuben, Reuben (De Vries) / A Mother's Kisses (Friedman) / Julian (Vidal) / Little Big Man (Berger) / In His Own Write (Lennon) / A Moveable Feast (Hemingway) / The Italians (Barzini) / Games People Play (Berne).

**Fads:** The see-through look / Animal shapes in jewelry.

## 1965

**World:** Winston Churchill, ninety, dies / Crop failure forces U.S.S.R. to buy wheat from Australia, Canada / Constantine II dismisses leftist Greek premier Papandreou / Rhodesia's prime minister declares independence from Britain / General Mobutu emerges as president of Congo Republic / U.S. sends troops to intervene in Dominican Republic civil war / Guinea alleges French plot to overthrow head of state / War rages between India, Pakistan.

**U.S.A.:** LBJ's state of the union speech calls for a "Great Society" / Dr. King leads Alabama "Freedom March" / Medicare enacted / Massive power failure in Northeast blacks out seven states / FTC rules cigarette packs must carry health warning / Federal Housing, Higher Education acts become law / Blacks riot in Los Angeles's Watts ghetto, National Guard restores order / Connecticut birth-control ban declared unconstitutional / Space program accelerates in series of Gemini, Pioneer missions.

**Vietnam:** U.S. lands first combat contingent, 3,500 marines, at Da Nang / Bomb wrecks U.S. embassy in Saigon / U.S.S.R. admits supplying arms to Hanoi / Planes bomb north in reprisal for Vietcong attacks on U.S. ground forces in south / Ho Chi Minh rejects LBJ proposal that UN negotiate peace / Johnson doubles monthly number of draftees, to 35,000 / Antiwar demonstrations increase.

**Firsts:** Man to walk in space (Leonov) / Black U.S. cabinet officer (Weaver, HUD) / Round-the-world flight over both poles / All-news radio programming (WINS, New York).

**Movies:** The Agony and the Ecstasy / Cat Ballou / The Greatest Story Ever Told / Help! / How to Murder Your Wife / The Ipcress File / King Rat / The Pawnbroker / Ship of Fools / The Spy Who Came in from the Cold / A Thousand Clowns / Thunderball / What's New, Pussycat? / Darling / Hush...Hush Sweet Charlotte / Juliet of the Spirits / Life at the Top / The Sandpiper / The Yellow Rolls-Royce / Those Magnificent Young Men in Their Flying Machines / The Sound of Music.

**Songs:** It's Not Unusual / My Girl / I Got You Babe / Hang On Sloopy / The Shadow of Your Smile / The Impossible Dream / Dulcinea / Do I Hear a Waltz? / Do You Believe in Magic? / Game of Love / Help! / Help Me, Rhonda / I Hear a Symphony / Satisfaction / Stop! In the Name of Love / Turn! Turn! Turn! / Sounds of Silence / What the World Needs Now Is Love / Like a Rolling Stone / Yesterday / Wooly Bully / Mrs. Brown You've Got a Lovely Daughter / Look of Love / You've Lost That Lovin' Feelin'.

**Stage:** The Odd Couple / The Right Honourable Gentleman / The Royal Hunt of the Sun / Inadmissible Evidence / Marat/Sade / Half a Sixpence / Flora, the Red Menace / The Roar of the Greasepaint—the Smell of the Crowd / Pickwick / On a Clear Day You Can See Forever / Man of La Mancha.

**Books:** The Source (Michener) / Hotel (Hailey) / An American Dream (Mailer) / The Looking Glass War (Le Carré) / Unsafe at Any Speed (Nader) / Kennedy (Sorensen) / A Thousand Days (Schlesinger) / The Making of the President, 1964 (White) / The Autobiography of Malcolm X (Haley) / The Kandy-Kolored Tangerine-Flake Streamline Baby (Wolfe) / Is Paris Burning? (Collins, Lapierre) / Manchild in the Promised Land (Brown).

**Fads:** The mod look / Op art fabrics / Being "in."

# 1966

**World:** U.S. bomber, tanker collide over Spain, lost H-bomb recovered by sub / Landslide engulfs Aberfan, Welsh mining community / Raging flood destroys Florence's age-old treasures / Guerrilla warfare persists on Israel's borders with Syria, Jordan / Upheaval, change affect Ghana, Guinea, Congo, South-West Africa, Bechuanaland, Basutoland / Verwoerd, architect of apartheid, assassinated by a white, Vorster takes over as prime minister / Junta overthrows Argentina's government / Mao launches cultural revolution / Indira Gandhi becomes India's prime minister.

**U.S.A.:** Supreme Court in *Miranda* decision curbs police interrogation powers / James Meredith, on lone march to boost black voter registration, shot in Mississippi / Madman mounts Austin, Texas, tower, wounds thirty-three, kills twelve / Chicago ex-convict rounds up nine nurses, kills them one by one / Daughter of U.S. Senator-to-Be Charles Percy victim of unsolved murder / Supreme Court upholds obscenity conviction of Ralph Ginzburg, publisher of *Eros*, but rules material of redeeming social value uncensorable / Ronald Reagan elected California governor.

**Vietnam:** U.S. cost for year totals $21 billion, troop count climbs to 389,000 / Bombings of north mount / Buddhists in south rebel, many self-immolate / U.S. attacks targets in Cambodia / North rejects peace overtures.

**Firsts:** Soft moon landing (*Luna IX*) / Soft Venus landing (*Venus III*) / Docking in space (*Gemini VIII*) / Medicare goes into effect / Black U.S. senator elected (Brooke, Massachusetts).

**Movies:** Dr. Zhivago / The Russians Are Coming... / Who's Afraid of Virginia Woolf? / Georgy Girl / A Man for All Seasons / Blow-Up / Alfie / Our Man Flint / Harper / Arabesque / Lady L / The Group / Born Free / This Property Is Condemned / Fantastic Voyage / Hawaii / The Fortune Cookie / Is Paris Burning? / Fahrenheit 451 / The Sand Pebbles / Funeral in Berlin / The Quiller Memorandum / Cul de Sac / Khartoum / Loves of a Blonde / Hotel Paradiso.

**Songs:** Born Free / Cabaret / Alfie / Eleanor Rigby / Georgy Girl / The Ballad of the Green Berets / California Dreamin' / Mame / If He Walked into My Life / Is That All There Is? / A Man and a Woman / Good Vibrations / Monday, Monday / A Groovy Kind of Love / On a Clear Day You Can See Forever / Over and Over / See You in September / Strangers in the Night / Sunny / Scarborough Fair / What Now, My Love? / Winchester Cathedral / Yellow Submarine / We Need a Little Christmas / Willkommen / Yesterday, When I Was Young.

**Stage:** A Lion in Winter / The Killing of Sister George / Don't Drink the Water / Wait Until Dark / Sweet Charity / Mame / Cabaret / I Do, I Do!

**Books:** Valley of the Dolls (Susann) / The Fixer (Malamud) / Tai-Pan (Clavell) / The Last Gentleman (Percy) / Human Sexual Response (Masters, Johnson) / In Cold Blood (Capote) / Rush to Judgment (Lane) / The Last Battle (Ryan) / Everything but Money (Levenson) / With Kennedy (Salinger) / Papa Hemingway (Hotchner) / A Choice of Weapons (Parks) / The Proud Tower (Tuchman) / The Battle of the Little Big Horn (Sandoz) / Inquest (Epstein).

**Fads:** Miniskirts / Paper jewelry, dresses / Transparent vinyl dresses / LSD / Batman / Topless waitresses / Pantsuits / Granny eyeglasses.

# 1967

**World:** Treaty among sixty-two nations limits military use of outer space / Cosmonaut dies in reentry crash / Stalin's daughter Svetlana gains U.S. asylum / Greek junta seizes power, king flees / Israel wins Six-Day War, defeating Egypt, Syria, Jordan / USS *Liberty* attacked by Israel in international waters, thirty-four die, seventy-five wounded / Congo premier Tshombe flees treason death sentence, hijackers fly plane to Algeria, hold him captive there / Cuban revolutionary Che Guevara killed by Bolivian troops / Red China tests H-bomb successfully, engages in border clashes with India / Expo 67 opens in Montreal.

**U.S.A.:** Race riots hit more than 100 cities during long, hot summer / House denies congressional seat to New York's Adam Clayton Powell for misuse of House funds; he wins reelection overwhelmingly / Teamster boss Jimmy Hoffa begins eight-year prison term / Jack Ruby, Oswald's killer, dies in jail / Astronauts Grissom, White, Chaffee killed in Apollo capsule fire / Time Inc. founder Henry R. Luce dies / Muhammad Ali appeals five-year sentence, fine for rejecting military service.

**Vietnam:** U.S. launches biggest offensive to date northwest of Saigon / Bombers based in Guam moved to Thailand / Losers charge election fraud as Nguyen Van Thieu, Nguyen Cao Ky take office as president, vice president / Thousands march on Washington in war protest.

**Firsts:** Black Supreme Court justice (Marshall) / Human heart transplant / Synthetic DNA / 3-D holograph movies.

**Movies:** In the Heat of the Night / Cool Hand Luke / In Cold Blood / Barefoot in the Park / Bonnie and Clyde / Casino Royale / A Countess from Hong Kong / The Dirty Dozen / Divorce American Style / Enter Laughing / Thoroughly Modern Millie / To Sir, with Love / The Way West / The Flim-Flam Man / The Night of the Generals / Ulysses / The Battle of Algiers / The Tiger Makes Out / You Only Live Twice / The Taming of the Shrew / La Guerre Est Finie / Elvira Madigan / Closely Watched Trains / Persona / Up the Down Staircase.

**Songs:** All You Need Is Love / By the Time I Get to Phoenix / The Beat Goes On / Can't Take My Eyes off of You / Daydream Believer / The 59th St. Bridge Song (Feelin' Groovy) / Gentle on My Mind / Alice's Restaurant / There's a Kind of Hush / Happy Together / It Must Be Him / Light My Fire / Michelle / Ode to Billy Joe / Penny Lane / Release Me / Ruby Tuesday / Somethin' Stupid / Up, Up and Away / Yesterday / Sgt. Pepper's Lonely Hearts Club Band.

**Stage:** Rosencrantz and Guildenstern Are Dead / There's a Girl in My Soup / MacBird! / Fortune and Men's Eyes / Scuba Duba / The Homecoming / You Know I Can't Hear You When the Water's Running / Hello, Dolly! (all-black cast) / Sherry / Hallelujah Baby.

**Books:** The Confessions of Nat Turner (Styron) / The Arrangement (Kazan) / The Chosen (Potok) / Topaz (Uris) / Rosemary's Baby (Levin) / Go to the Widow-Maker (Jones) / Washington, D.C. (Vidal) / The Manor (Singer) / Incredible Victory (Lord) / Our Crowd (Birmingham) / Nicholas and Alexandra (Massie) / Division Street, America (Terkel) / The New Industrial State (Galbraith) / Why Are We in Vietnam? (Mailer) / Death of a President (Manchester) / The Gabriel Hounds (Stewart).

**Fads:** The Twiggy look / Posters / 3-D ticktacktoe.

## 1968

**World:** Czechs institute liberal reforms; 200,000 Soviet, Warsaw Pact troops invade, force repeal / UN General Assembly condemns apartheid, Portugal's colonial policies in Africa / Trudeau becomes Canada's prime minister / U.S. bomber carrying unarmed H-bombs crashes in Greenland / Israeli commandos raid Beirut airport following border clashes with Lebanon / Aswan Dam completed / Mexico City hosts Olympic Games / USS *Pueblo*, Intelligence ship, seized by North Korea, held for year / Papal encyclical bars all artificial means of contraception.

**U.S.A.:** LBJ announces he will not seek reelection / Martin Luther King, Jr., Robert F. Kennedy assassinated / Blacks riot in many cities / 10,000 antiwar protesters clash with police, National Guardsmen at Democrats' convention in Chicago / Nixon-Agnew ticket defeats Humphrey-Muskie / Students create campus turmoil nationally, demonstrating against university investment policies, government involvement in Vietnam / Congress passes Truth in Lending Act / Poor People's March on capital protests hunger / Kerner Commission cites white racism as major cause of civil disorder by blacks / César Chavez organizes nationwide grape boycott to win gains for farm workers.

**Vietnam:** In Tet offensive Communists attack 100 towns, bases / Siege of garrison at Khe Sanh lifted after seventy-six days / Preliminary peace talks begin in Paris / Bombardments of north halted / Opposition to war mounts.

**Firsts:** Supersonic airliner / Manned moon orbit / Black to win men's U.S. Tennis Open (Ashe).

**Movies:** Bullitt / 2001 / Guess Who's Coming to Dinner / The Graduate / The Heart Is a Lonely Hunter / The Lion in Winter / The Odd Couple / Planet of the Apes / The Producers / Rachel, Rachel / Rosemary's Baby / The Subject Was Roses / The Thomas Crown Affair / I Love You, Alice B. Toklas / The Good, the Bad and the Ugly / Finian's Rainbow / Funny Girl / Oliver! / The Yellow Submarine.

**Songs:** The Dock of the Bay / Hey, Jude / Little Green Apples / Hair / Good Morning, Starshine / Aquarius / MacArthur Park / Mrs. Robinson / I Say a Little Prayer / This Guy's in Love with You / Wichita Lineman / The Windmills of Your Mind / Harper Valley P.T.A. / Folsom Prison Blues / Those Were the Days / Abraham, Martin and John / Jumpin' Jack Flash / As I Went Out One Morning / Grazin' in the Grass / Lady Madonna.

**Stage:** Plaza Suite / The Man in the Glass Booth / The Great White Hope / The Prime of Miss Jean Brodie / I Never Sang for My Father / A Day in the Death of Joe Egg / The Boys in the Band / Lovers and Other Strangers / Hair / Zorba / Jacques Brel Is Alive and Well....

**Books:** The Day Kennedy Was Shot (Bishop) / Airport (Hailey) / True Grit (Portis) / Myra Breckinridge (Vidal) / Couples (Updike) / Preserve and Protect (Drury) / Welcome to the Monkey House (Vonnegut) / The Armies of the Night (Mailer) / The Electric Kool-Aid Acid Test (Wolfe) / Slouching Towards Bethlehem (Didion) / Soul on Ice (Cleaver) / The Double Helix (Watson) / The Naked Ape (Morris) / The Algiers Motel Incident (Hersey) / Tell Me How Long the Train's Been Gone (Baldwin).

**Fads:** Unisex clothing / Gold-chain necklaces.

## 1969

**World:** SALT talks begin in Helsinki / Civil strife mounts in Northern Ireland / De Gaulle resigns, Pompidou succeeds him as president / Brandt heads Socialist regime in Bonn / Giant oil field discovered in North Sea / Golda Meir becomes Israel's premier / Arafat elected PLO chairman / Captain Gaddafi, in military coup, assumes control of Libya / Nationalist rebels in Angola, Mozambique, Guinea fight Portuguese / El Salvador, Honduras in undeclared war / Military commanders take over in Brazil, Bolivia / Antigovernment riots in Pakistan lead to resignation of President Ayub Khan / Ho Chi Minh dies.

**U.S.A.:** James Earl Ray gets ninety-nine years for killing Dr. King / Sirhan Sirhan convicted for RFK slaying / Eisenhower dies / Senator Ted Kennedy's career blighted following auto accident on Chappaquiddick Island / Rock festivals at Woodstock, New York, and Altamont, California, draw 300,000 each / Supreme Court justice Abe Fortas, under fire for ties to stock manipulator, resigns / Nixon appoints Warren Burger chief justice / Trial begins of Chicago Eight, protest leaders at 1968 Democratic convention / Campus demonstrations spread / Miracle New York Mets win World Series.

**Vietnam:** Vietcong, South Vietnamese join U.S.-North Vietnam representatives in Paris peace talks / Nixon announces phased troop withdrawal / My Lai massacre revealed / Mass Moratorium Day demonstrations held nationwide.

**Firsts:** Man on moon (Armstrong) / Human in vitro fertilization / Supersonic passenger jet flight (Concorde) / Implantation of artificial heart in human / Giant passenger jet (747).

**Movies:** Midnight Cowboy / True Grit / The Love Bug / Alice's Restaurant / The Wild Bunch / The Secret of Santa Vittoria / Easy Rider / Goodbye, Columbus / Bob & Carol & Ted & Alice / Butch Cassidy and the Sundance Kid / The Sterile Cuckoo / Take the Money and Run / Royal Hunt of the Sun / Stolen Kisses / Tell Them Willie Boy Is Here / I Am Curious (Yellow) / Downhill Racer / The Prime of Miss Jean Brodie / Marlowe / Chitty Chitty Bang Bang.

**Songs:** Come Saturday Morning / I'll Never Fall in Love Again / Raindrops Keep Fallin' on My Head / Leaving on a Jet Plane / Lay Lady Lay / A Boy Named Sue / Games People Play / Get Back / Honky Tonk Women / Hurt So Bad / I've Gotta Be Me / Sugar, Sugar / Wedding Bell Blues.

**Stage:** Butterflies Are Free / Play It Again, Sam / Ceremonies in Dark Old Men / To Be Young, Gifted and Black / 1776 / Oh Calcutta! / Promises, Promises / Celebration.

**Books:** The Godfather (Puzo) / The Love Machine (Susann) / Slaughterhouse Five (Vonnegut) / Portnoy's Complaint (Roth) / The Inheritors (Robbins) / The Andromeda Strain (Crichton) / Ada (Nabokov) / Bullet Park (Cheever) / The First Circle (Solzhenitsyn) / Force 10 from Navarone (MacLean) / Naked Came the Stranger ("Ashe") / The Making of the President 1968 (White) / The Selling of the President 1968 (McGinniss) / The Valachi Papers (Maas) / An Unfinished Woman (Hellman) / Ernest Hemingway: A Life Story (Baker) / The Collapse of the Third Republic (Shirer) / The 900 Days (Salisbury) / The Kingdom and the Power (Talese) / Grant Takes Command (Catton) / The Arms of Krupp (Manchester) / The Season (Goldman).

**Fads:** Bell-bottom pants / Couples in unisex outfits.

# Photographers

*The role of Time Inc.'s Photo Lab and Picture Collection in reproducing, indexing, and preserving hundreds of thousands of photographs by LIFE photographers and others is an essential factor in the creation of books such as this one. The fulfillment of this role, at a consistently high level of quality, calls for skill and knowledge. The staffs of both the Photo Lab and Picture Collection bring these qualities in abundance to their work, together with a rare sense of dedication.*